Memoirs of a Korean Queen

Yang-hi Choe-Wall was born in Seoul, Korea, the fourth child of a family whose head was a distinguished professor of English literature. Dr Choe-Wall taught English at high school and university in Korea before moving to Canberra, Australia, where she completed her M.A. and Ph.D. at the Australian National University. She is currently lecturer in Korean language in the China Centre at ANU. Her field of interest is Korean literature of the early and mid Yi dynasty.

Memoirs of a Korean Queen

Lady Hong

Edited, introduced and translated
by Choe-Wall Yang-hi

KPI
LONDON AND NEW YORK

First published in 1985 by KPI Ltd.
This edition published in 1987 by KPI Ltd,
11 New Fetter Lane, London EC4P 4EE

Distributed by Routledge & Kegan Paul,
Associated Book Publishers (UK) Ltd
11 New Fetter Lane, London EC4P 4EE

Methuen Inc., Routledge & Kegan Paul
29 West 35th Street, New York, NY 10001, USA

Printed in Great Britain
by T. J. Press (Padstow) Ltd.,
Padstow, Cornwall

Korean Culture Series
ISBN 0-7103-0248-7 (paperback)
ISBN 0-7103-0052-2 (cased)

Contents

Preface

This book is a revision of a thesis submitted some years ago to the Australian National University in Canberra as part of the requirements for the degree of Master of Arts. The thesis, *Hanjung nok* with Introduction and Annotation, is housed in the University Library. Those readers who desire a fuller translation with detailed annotations and appendices are referred to it.

Both Professor A. L. Basham, then Head of the Department of Asian Civilizations at the Australian National University, and my thesis supervisor Dr K. H. J. Gardiner encouraged me to rewrite the work and adapt it for the general reader, and I am grateful to them for their help and guidance.

My most heartfelt thanks are also due to Dr J. Brewster for her great help with the revision and subsequent composition. I am particularly indebted to her.

Finally, my acknowledgements would not be complete without special reference to my family. My husband, Ray, gave his constant support and invaluable co-operation. My children, Dai kyu and Mikyung, showed a marked degree of patience during the preparation of both thesis and book. Without it, this book could not have been written.

Yang-hi Choe-Wall

For Ray

Editorial Notes

In order to keep the narrative as clear as possible, most important official titles are given English translations. Persons mentioned in the text are listed with dates, offices held and other details in Appendix I. In Appendix II maps are provided of the Court at the time of King Yŏngio, as an aid to following the many references to places.

All Korean words used in this narrative are transliterated according to the system of McCune-Reischauer.

In this translation the mark ‿ has been translated as · throughout.

Introduction

The memoir of Lady Hong of Hyegyŏng Palace (*Hanjung nok*, 1796) is one of the rare historical examples of literary composition by a Korean woman of the Yi dynasty (1392–1910).

A product of neo-Confucian court society of the late eighteenth century, this autobiographical memoir gives a vivid account of court life in the time of King Yŏngjo (reigned 1725–1776). Not only a touching description of the tragic incidents involving Lady Hong's family, it is also a valuable disclosure of the rigidity of the royal court, as well as a vital historical source. Its elegant prose and insight into human behaviour is seldom found in works by male authors of the same period. The memoir is also one of the few works of the time written in *han'gŭl*, the Korean alphabet. It is a significant and precious record of the life of one who was compelled to obey the discipline and etiquette of the court, as decreed by the male rulers who were moulded by neo-Confucian philosophy.

Born the daughter of the president of the state council, Hong Pong-han (1713–1778), Lady Hong (1735–1815) became the wife of Crown Prince Sado (1735–1762) when she was ten years old. At the time of her wedding, the crown prince was in line to become the twenty-second king of the Yi dynasty. Isolated from the world outside the palace walls, she led an austere existence, with few consolations. Yet, despite her initial apprehension, she gradually became accustomed to the strict etiquette which the court imposed. For the first ten years of her marriage, her life was relatively stable and she bore the crown prince two daughters and a son — later to become King Chŏngjo (reigned 1776–1800). She was happy as a wife and mother, but her well-being was later shattered by tragic circumstances she was powerless to prevent.

Lady Hong's memoir shows that, as a woman of the court, she held an inferior position. Despite this, her fortitude and extreme devotion to her family, especially to a husband who was increasingly mentally unstable, under the onslaught of King Yŏngjo's growing anger, rank her as an outstanding woman of her time. The crown prince's early death, at the hand of his father, is dealt with in the memoir with the controlled emotion and compassion which permeates the whole of her work. Despite the suffering and tragedy she had to bear, she remained a model of Confucian virtue.

All record of the crown prince's death, known as the Imo Incident, after the year in which it took place (1762), was deleted from the diary of the royal secretariat at the request of King Chŏngjo. Privately-written accounts of the incident were subsequently produced which gave different descriptions of it. Lady Hong's memoir was begun in 1796 when she was in her sixtieth year, and completed when she was seventy-one. This translation is based on the first three chapters of the collated *Ilsa* and *Karam* manuscript collections, reprinted under the title of *Handyung nok*, in Seoul in 1961. The Imo Incident was recorded to inform Lady Hong's grandson, young King Sunjo (reigned 1800–1834), of the facts of the tragedy that had befallen his grandfather, and thus to condition him from blaming her family, which had been unjustly accused of being the prime instigator of the killing.

Like most upper-class women, Lady Hong's education rested heavily on a thorough indoctrination in the requirements of virtuous conduct as laid down in the Chinese classics. The twentieth-century reader is fortunate that despite the restrictions placed on her by Confucian ethics, she learned to read and write and that her memoir has survived to give us a remarkably clear insight into an important period of Korean literature.

Chapter I

I was a mere child when I came to the court, and wrote twice a day to my parents. However, none of this correspondence has survived, because at the time my father warned me not to leave my mother's letters lying about the court, nor to write at too great length myself, but rather to send back a short greeting appended to each note from my mother. This I did, and once the note, with my few words of greeting, had been read by my parents, the brush-strokes were erased.

My nephew Su-yòng kept begging me to write some sort of record which would be kept as a family heirloom. He thought this would be an admirable undertaking, and I quite agreed with him, but I never seemed to find the time to carry out the idea. Now, however, I am in my sixtieth year, and while the passing of the years seems rather to have intensified the pain I feel at recollections of my late lord, nevertheless my memory will merely get weaker with the passage of time. And so I am setting down all those old experiences and thoughts, although I fear I can only recall a small fraction of them.

I was born during the reign of King Yòngjo, at noon on 6 August 1735, at my mother's family home in Kòp'yòng-dong, Pangsong-bang. One night, before I was born, my father had dreamed of a black dragon coiled around the rafters of my mother's room, but the birth of a daughter did not seem to fit the portent of his dream.

My paternal grandfather, Lord Chòng-hòn, came to look at me, and took an immediate fancy to me, declaring, 'Although it is a girl, this is no ordinary child!' As I grew up, he became so fond of me that he was reluctant to let me leave his lap. He would say jokingly, 'This girl is quite a little lady already, so she is sure to grow up quickly!'

When I was three weeks old, mother returned with me to the family home. There my great-grandmother, Lady Yi, saw me, and was filled with high hopes for my future. 'This child is no ordinary girl,' she said. 'Be sure to bring her up very carefully.' She set about arranging a wet nurse for me.

When I came to the court, I recalled the prophecies of these two generations of grandparents, and although I did not enjoy court life, my future somehow seemed linked to their words.

I had one sister, and my parents treasured us like two precious jewels. However my sister died very young, and so all my parents' affection was lavished on me. They brought me up very strictly, and my eldest brother — your father — also helped in my upbringing. My father had a special tenderness for me, because I was a girl, and I, for my part, used to feel completely lost when he was away. I always tried to be close to both my parents, and with increasing maturity I strove to return their tremendous love by never causing them the least anxiety. Although I could never truly repay them, being a girl, I was still deeply and sincerely grateful for all they had done for me. Whenever I recall their great love for me, I feel a lump in my throat, for I cannot help feeling that the intensity of their love was somehow preordained, as was the fact that they were to lose me so soon to the palace.

Our family is descended from a royal son-in-law, and belongs to a great clan which has produced generations of senior government officials. My grandfather, Lord Chŏng-hŏn was the great-grandson of the royal son-in-law Prince Yongan, and grandson of Lord Chŏng-gan. As the second son of Lord Ch'ŏm-jŏng, he built a separate mansion in An'guk-dong, and established a cadet family. Although the house looked as splendid as that of a court minister, life was difficult there, since he received only a very small share of the family fortune. Still, he was well treated by my great-uncle who was a deputy board minister. When my father was a child, the latter used to pat him on the head and say that he was like Yun O-ŭm,[1] and that although he was then very poor, he was destined to be an exceptional man who would one day be very rich. For, from ancient times, those destined to lasting happiness in their later years have felt obliged to endure hardships in their youth.

Accordingly my great-uncle did not share the family fortune with his brother but rather loved him from a distance, and was praised by the entire family for this behaviour. But in our case circumstances were very difficult. Grandfather, though minister of the board of rites, was a very upright and honest man with no great career ambitions, and his house was quiet and unfrequented, like that of a poor scholar.

Grandfather's second wife was the daughter of a Confucian scholar, and consequently well-educated. She was a clever, virtuous and gracious woman, who treated her husband with the respect due to an important guest. She ran the household plainly, in keeping with her husband's principles. This was the reason why my mother, although married to the eldest son of a ministerial family, had not even one silk garment hanging in her closet, very few jewels in her jewel-box, and only one set of clothes for each season. When these clothes became soiled she would make no fuss about washing them herself at night. She also wove her own cotton cloth and did all her own sewing. As she disliked being praised for her diligence by the maidservants, she would cover the windows with cloth, so that her light could not been seen, and would continue working late into the cold night, until her hands were worn. She dressed us children as she did herself, in very plain cotton, but the clothes were always clean and in keeping with the season. You can imagine from all this how frugal and tidy she was. But though uncompromising in these respects, she had a placid nature and was not lightly moved to joy or anger.

The womenfolk of our family were all connected with the most respected clans of the day. My mother came from the Yi family — an upright clan. My father's eldest sister was married to a famous magistrate; while his second sister was a daughter-in-law of Prince Ch'ŏng-nŭng; and his youngest sister a daughter-in-law of the minister of the board of civil office. Despite these connections, they were not haughty or extravagant, as is so often the case. When the family gathered together on festival days, my mother always treated the elder members with respect, and greeted the younger ones with a kind smile and an affectionate word. Father's second brother's wife was likewise virtuous, and her esteem for my mother was exceeded only by that for her mother-in-law. She was an outstanding woman — noble-minded and well educated. She was very fond of me; taught me my Korean alphabet and instructed me in a wide range of subjects. I loved her like a mother, and indeed mother used to say that I had grown too close to her.

Grandfather died in 1740, and I was much affected by my father's distress. He made offerings at his father's shrine twice daily for three years, and afterwards erected a memorial tablet. Although I was too young to understand all this, I shall certainly never forget the filial piety my father displayed towards his ancestors. He was a model of filial behaviour, visiting the shrine early every morning, and then going to see his stepmother, bowing to her and comforting her with gentle words and little acts of kindness. Everyone said grandmother loved him and expected more of him than she would have done if he had been her own child. He was devoted to his two elder sisters, and also did all he could to help in the upbringing of his three younger brothers. He could not have done more if he was grandmother's own son.

In 1741 his eldest sister contracted an infectious disease. Her blood relatives hurriedly left, all except my father, who looked after her, saying, 'If one does not help one's own brothers and sisters when they are sick, how can one presume to call oneself brother or sister.' After her death he went to see her family and undertook the arrangements for the funeral. After the funeral, he did all he could for her bereaved children, and brought one of her daughters to our house and arranged her marriage.

So you can see that his love and concern for his relatives went well beyond the normal. Furthermore, he often invited my two aunts, his two eldest sisters, the wives of Yi *Chinsa*[2] and Yi Namp'yŏng, to our house. This will all help you to understand how seriously he regarded his filial duties. He had been brought up by his grandmother, and had never missed the performance of a single rite for her, mourning her like one of his own parents. Even as a child, I respected him for all this. He always studied hard and read with famous scholars, and often when the lesson was over, he would bring his teacher and friends home with him.

After grandfather's death in 1740, mother performed the special memorial services for the ancestors for three years, in accordance with the dictates of ritual. She prepared all the offerings herself and followed the prescribed customs, waking up early in the morning, washing her face, combing her hair, and greeting her mother-in-law at the approved time every day. She would always put her hair up before she went to see her mother-in-law and would attire herself in a formal jacket. She respected and helped her husband, far more than most women, which led him to hold her in high esteem.

4

Mother was married at Haeju in Hwanghae province in 1727, and lost her father shortly thereafter. She went to her husband's home the following year, as it would not have been proper for her to go to her parents-in-law's house while in mourning. In 1738 she lost her mother, which also brought her great sorrow. Whenever she had to come back home after a visit to her mother's house — and such visits could never last long enough for her — she and her brother would weep. Her family was well-known for its integrity, and affection between brothers and sisters came naturally. Even the women in the family got on very well together. Lady Hong, the wife of my mother's brother, Lord Chi-rye, would entertain her young sisters-in-law most graciously whenever they visited her. I myself was a favourite with Uncle Chi-rye, as well as with the family of my cousin Sanjung.

Mother was one of three sisters. One had married *Saengwŏn*[3] Kim, but was widowed very early in life. Mother was devoted to her, and after his death felt so sorry for the children that she treated them as lovingly as her own. She fed and clothed them, and later even helped to arrange their marriages. My cousins used to say, 'Everyone in the world has a mother, but we have two.'

When my cousin, Kim I-gi, was to be married in the late spring of 1741 at my mother's family home, mother went there to make preparations for the ceremony. The daughter of mother's other sister, the wife of the deputy board minister Song, was married to my youngest uncle. We used to play together as children when we visited our mother's family home. She arrived at cousin Kim's wedding, attired in her gayest costume, whereas I was wearing white, even though I was still too young to wear mourning clothes. Mother said, 'Your cousin looks so nice. Let's dress you like her.'

I replied, 'I don't think I can dress as prettily as that, because I am in mourning.' I refused to go out of the gate, but stayed close beside my mother. My behaviour showed the effect of my parents' constant admonitions, for I was too young to really understand the situation for myself.

In the third month, 1743, father was made a senior student of the Confucian Academy, and summoned to an audience with the king. He was then 31, of noble disposition and bearing. He was foremost among the scholars of the Confucian Academy, and there was no mistake in his answers to the king's questions. The king was most impressed, and after paying homage at the Confucian temple, he asked the Confucian scholars to sit a state examination. We all imagined that the king fully intended father to pass. My uncle came home to wait for the publication of the results. Incredibly, father failed, and I, waiting at home, wept with disappointment. That autumn, father was appointed custodian of one of the royal tombs, and for the first time since 1740, our family was blessed with an official salary. The whole family rejoiced, and mother shared out the entire supply of rice amongst our relatives.

In 1743 came an edict requesting officials to submit the names of their daughters so that a wife might be selected for the crown prince. It was said that it would do no harm if a poor scholar did not report his daughter, in order to avoid the expense of preparing a costume. However, father submitted my name on the grounds that he was a serving official from a family which had seen generations of government service, and that his daughter was the grandchild of a minister. He would not therefore deceive the government by failing to report. The family was really too poor to prepare the special clothes. I can still see my mother slaving to prepare the costume: she made my skirt out of the material she had been saving for my late sister's marriage, and lined it with used material. She had to borrow money for the rest of the outfit.

The first selection was on 13 November 1743. King Yŏngjo praised my meagre talents and showed me special favour. Queen Chŏngsŏng looked me over very closely. The crown prince's mother Lady Sŏnhŭi, was not permitted to be present at the selection, but she called me in beforehand. Her face filled with delight on seeing me, and she took an instant liking to me. The court ladies all embraced me.

Meantime I received presents from the king, and Lady Sŏnhŭi and Princess Hwap'yŏng instructed me in court etiquette. I did everything I was taught. That night, when I came back from court, I slept in my mother's arms. Early next morning, father came in and said agitatedly to my mother, 'What can we do? The child came first.'

Mother too was disturbed and said 'Since she is only the daughter of a poor scholar, it would have been better not to have reported her name.'

I overheard this conversation from under the bedclothes, and was most upset and cried a lot. When I remembered how the court ladies had been so kind to me, I was shocked and unhappy. My parents said I was too young to understand these things but I was very depressed after that first selection. It must have been because

I was fated to experience so many shifts of fortune at the court. It all seemed very strange to me, and yet somehow I felt that I understood everything quite clearly.

After that first selection, our family was visited by all sorts of people, from all ranks of life — men whose steps had not turned towards our house for a long time. This revealed to me the ways of the world, of life and of men.

The second selection was on 13 December. Naturally I was more frightened this time than I had been before, when my parents had sent me to court hoping that I would not be selected. When I arrived at court, it appeared that the decision to choose me had already been made. Quarters were allocated to me near the royal presence, and I was treated differently from all the others. I was completely bewildered. Then, when I entered the royal presence, King Yŏngjo treated me quite differently from the others, coming inside the screen and patting me on the head. He said, 'I keep remembering your grandfather, and how delighted I was to encounter your father. Just fancy you being his daughter!' He was very pleased.

Queen Chŏngsŏng and Lady Sŏnhŭi seemed to have taken a liking to me, and all the princesses took me by the hand. They did not send me home straight away. Instead I stayed at the Kyŏngch'un-jŏn Mansion, so that I would make a more dignified appearance, and my midday meal was served there. A court lady tried to take off my ceremonial coat to measure me, but I refused to let her do so. At last she persuaded me, but I was so frightened I wanted to cry. However, I managed to hold back the tears until I was in the palanquin taking me home. I was frightened again when the men servants were carrying out my palanquin, and I saw a black-costumed maid, one of those who carry royal messages.

When I arrived home, my palanquin was brought in through the guests' entrance, and my father came to help me out, attired in full dress. Both he and mother looked so confused, and were so deferential, that I burst into tears and hugged them both. Mother was also in ceremonial dress, and had covered the table with a red cloth. She behaved very properly, bowing four times on receiving the queen's letter, and twice on receiving Lady Sŏnhŭi's.

After that, my parents addressed me differently using respectful forms of speech. All the family elders, too, treated me with respect, to my great embarrassment. My father, anxious and fearful, kept on instructing me and warning me about so many things, that I felt I had committed some crime, and wished I could hide myself away. I was heartbroken at the prospect of having to leave my parents, and could take no interest in anything.

In the meantime, every single member of the family came to visit me before I finally left for court. The more distant relatives were entertained by my parents in the guest room, and seen off without meeting me. But I dutifully saw in person all those descended from my own great-grandparents. One of the more distant relatives warned me that court life was strict, and that once inside the palace it would be farewell forever. He urged me to be careful and respectful. He added, 'My name is *Kam* for mirror and *Po* for assistant. Please remember me after you get to the court.' Although I had never seen him before, I was saddened by what he said.

The third selection was on 28 December, and as it approached I was overcome with sadness, and slept in my mother's arms at night. Father's two sisters and my uncle's wife made much of me and were depressed about my (coming) departure. My parents lavished affection on me day and night. They were so unhappy that they would not sleep for nights on end. Even now, my heart aches at the memory.

After the second selection, Governess Ch'oe and Miss Kim Hyodŏk were sent to our place to take care of me. Governess Ch'oe was a large, imposing woman, not like the usual delicate court lady. She had served the court for several reigns, and mother entertained her especially warmly. She measured me for my costume, and returned before the third selection, accompanied by Miss Mun Tae-bok. They brought costumes prepared by Queen Chŏngsŏng: a formal green silk coat, a pair of jackets — one of creamy silk with a grape pattern and the other of violet silk; a crimson patterned silk shirt; and a jacket of ramie cloth.

I had never been dressed so prettily before, but then I had never wanted to dress like all the other girls. Among my close relatives, for instance, there was a girl of my age whose family was very rich. Her parents cherished her dearly, and lavished on her practically every fine dress you could imagine, but I never felt jealous of her. One day she visited us looking very pretty, wearing a deep red skirt lined with the same material. Mother asked me if I would like to wear something similar.

'If I had something like that, I would be stupid not to wear it, but I don't especially want it,' I replied.

Mother was very moved, and said 'You only say that because

you were born into a poor family. I will reward you by making you a beautiful skirt when you get married.'

Now she wept, because the situation was changed, and declared 'Since I never dressed you prettily in gay clothes, I want to make a skirt for you now, and dress you up in it before you go to the court, for you won't be able to wear ordinary clothes once you are there.' So sadly she made my skirt between the second and third selections, and I wept as I put it on.

I thought I ought to say farewell to the main shrine of my father's family, and at the shrine of mother's parents, and received the king's permission to do so. My request was conveyed to Lady Sŏnhŭi, and thence to the king, by my second aunt's sister-in-law, who was the wife of the elder brother of the royal son-in-law, Prince Kŭmsŏng. I went to the principal mansion of my father's family in a palanquin, accompanied by my mother. I had often stayed there with father's cousin and his wife, for they had no daughter of their own, and loved me as if I were their own. The king was aware of this, and had ordered father's cousin to instruct my family in the marriage rituals. Once it was decided that I should marry the crown prince, father's cousin had come to stay at our house. So now only his wife was at home to welcome mother and myself, and guide me to the shrine where I was to pay my respects to the ancestral tablets. According to custom, descendants are supposed to bow to the shrine kneeling on the ground, but I was frightened enough merely bowing in the main hall of the house.

I also went the same day to mother's parents' home, where I was welcomed by my uncle's wife, who was sad to be losing me. My cousins used once to carry me on their backs and in their arms, but now they remained at a discreet distance, and behaved very respectfully, which made me feel very sad. I was very fond of my cousin, Madame Sin, and felt depressed at the thought of leaving her behind. I visited mother's two sisters, and then returned home, for the day of the third selection was drawing near.

Father's sisters wanted me to visit all my blood relatives and took me visiting on the night of the twenty-seventh. It was a pleasant, moonlit night, but cold, with the wind blowing over the snow. My aunt took me from one house to another, holding my hand in hers, while tears ran down my cheeks.

Once back home, in the privacy of my room, I tried to control my feelings, and did not sleep a wink all night. Early next morning the others urged me to hurry and set out for the palace. The womenfolk

9

of our distant relatives had come to our home that day to say goodbye, and close relatives were ready to escort me to the Detached Palace. When I performed the ritual farewell at the family shrine, father had difficulty reading the prayer because of the tears which kept welling up. I cannot express how sad everyone was at my departure.

My first stop was the Kyŏngch'un-jŏn Mansion, where I rested from my journey, before proceeding to the T'ongmyŏng-jŏn Mansion where I was presented before the king and queen, and the Queen Dowager Inwŏn. It was my first meeting with the queen dowager, who said, 'She is very beautiful and good-natured. How lucky our state is!'

King Yŏngjo was very glad to see me, repeating his earlier sentiment, 'What a lucky day it was when I decided to choose such a sensible girl!'

Queen Chŏngsŏng was delighted to see me, and Lady Sŏnhŭi showed me such affection, that I felt a surge of respect for them both. They rearranged my hair, and touched up my face. Then I sat down in ceremonial costume at the dinner table prepared for me. Soon after dark, I bowed four times to the three royal highnesses, and left for the Detached Palace. King Yŏngjo himself escorted me to my palanquin, and said, 'Keep well, and come back soon.' He also told me, as he held my hands in his, that he would send a copy of the *Hsiao-hsüeh* (*Sohak* in Korean)[4] for me to study with father. When I reached the Detached Palace, having thus received proof of the king's constant affection for me, it was quite dark and the lights were lit.

I could not get to sleep that night, for court ladies were sleeping on either side of me, and I was frightened and miserable at having to sleep away from my mother, which I knew affected her too. Governess Ch'oe, who was an uncompromising woman with no concern for the feelings of others, had told mother that it was now against the laws of the land for her to sleep beside me any more, and that she should go to her bedroom. It was heartless of her, and I was quite unable to sleep.

Next day the king sent over the *Hsiao-hsüeh*, and from then on my father taught me this text every day. This class was joined by father's cousin, father's two younger brothers, the younger of whom was still a child, and my brother. The king also sent the instruction manual containing the prose pieces he had written for Queen Hyosun.[5] I was supposed to read this in my spare time between the *Hsiao-hsüeh* lessons.

Amongst the furnishings of the Detached Palace was a big aubergine-shaped Japanese pearl given me by Lady Sŏnhŭi. It had belonged to Princess Chŏngmyŏng, who had given it to her grandchild Madame Cho. Apparently it had thereafter been sold, and Lady Sŏnhŭi had bought it through one of her court ladies. I felt that it was not mere chance that I, a descendant of the princess, had come to the palace and received her pearl.

My grandfather, Lord Chŏnghŏn, had been very fond of calligraphy and painting, and had owned an embroidered gold folding screen in four panels. After his death in 1740, it had been sold by one of the servants. By chance, Lady Sŏnhŭi bought it through one of the relatives of her court maid, and sent it to me so that I could have it in my bedroom. One of father's younger sisters remarked how strange it was to see the folding screen which used to belong to her father now gracing the bedroom of his grand-daughter at the royal palace.

Lady Sŏnhŭi also sent me her own folding screen, featuring an embroidered dragon, and this too I set up in my bedroom. On seeing it father said that the colour of the dragon was the same as that he had seen in his dream on the eve of my birth in 1735. On waking, he had been unable to recall what the dragon looked like, but now, seeing this one on the screen, he recollected that the dragon in his dream had been just like it. Everyone was surprised by this correspondence between the embroidered dragon and the one of father's dream. The scales of this dragon were embroidered with golden thread on a black background and the combination gave the impression of movement. Father, who had never been quite certain that the dragon he had dreamed of had been black, now recalled that it had been like this.

During the first fifty days I spent at the Detached Palace, the three royal ladies would send Governess Ch'oe to see how I was. Each time she came, she sought an interview with my family and treated them with deep respect, for which I was very grateful. As soon as she arrived, the officer of ceremony would appear with a table of wine and food. The food was so abundant and the entertainment so hospitable that it was the talk of the entire court at my wedding in 1744.

While I was staying at the Detached Palace, my grandmother fell seriously ill. My parents were most anxious and agitated, for her condition was grave, and the royal wedding was drawing near. It would have been very hard for them to leave me at such a time, even if they had had no other worries. However, in spite of their anxieties, they never failed to appear content whenever they came to visit me at the Detached Palace. When they had to move grandmother to another place for her safety, father carried her out on his back to the palanquin. The court ladies were most impressed when they heard of this, and praised him highly for his filial piety towards his stepmother. Fortunately, grandmother recovered, which was indeed a blessing for the country as well as for my family. I still think I have never been so anxious as during those days.

On 21 February 1744, I was formally invested as wife of the crown prince, and the wedding took place two days later. As the wedding day approached, I wept constantly at the thought of leaving my parents. Although they must have felt very sad, they bore it well, and father warned me, 'When the family of a subject of the king becomes royal relatives, they gain the favour of the king and prosper. But such prosperity invites evils. Our family, being descended from a royal son-in-law, won boundless favour one generation after another, and I would never refuse to undertake a task, however difficult, for the good of the country. But when a scholar with very little experience of the world suddenly becomes a royal relative, it is an omen, not of happiness, but of the beginning of misfortunes. It worries me greatly that I do not know what to do!' He gave me detailed instructions, saying, 'Revere the king, the queen and the queen dowager, and devote yourself to them. Help and guide the crown prince in the right paths, talking carefully and making every possible effort for the happiness of your family and country.'

Although I listened respectfully to his countless words of warning, I could not stop weeping. Even the most insensitive being would have been moved on such an occasion. After the marriage ceremony, my parents again instructed me and warned me about various matters while I listened respectfully. At the time father was wearing deep crimson official clothes and his scholar's hat, mother was also in ceremonial dress, with her hair formally arranged. All our relatives had gathered to see me off, as well as lots of people from the court. My parents conducted everything so modestly, solemnly and properly, that everyone who saw them praised him and declared that the country had found a wonderful (royal) father-in-law.

After the wedding, I entered the palace, where the wedding

reception was held, and on 24 February 1744 I had an audience with the king, who said, 'Since I have now received your bridal gifts, let me give you some advice. Be gentle with the crown prince, neither talking flippantly, nor frivolously changing the colour of your face. In our court there are many ordinary things which may appear unusual to you. You should pretend not to have seen them.' I accepted these warnings with respect.

On the same day, the king, queen and Lady Sŏnhŭi gave an audience to my father at the T'ongmyŏng-jŏn Mansion. They talked very kindly to him, and offered him a cup of wine. Father accepted it, drank some, poured the remainder into his sleeve; and placed some citrus seeds from the table in his bosom. The king told me that my father showed great understanding of the rules of behaviour. Father was moved to tears by this, and withdrew to tell the family that for such royal favours they should be prepared to forfeit their lives.

Next day the king held audience for all the government officials at his residential palace so that they would see me and my family. After the audience, I went to the Taejo-jŏn Mansion to pay my respects. Queen Chŏngsŏng was very courteous towards my mother, treating her just as the parents of a middle-class mother might have treated each other. She told my mother how noble it was of her to have produced so beautiful a daughter and that the kingdom would enjoy the happiness of this wedding. Queen Dowager Inwŏn sent a governess to entertain us. Although she did not meet us in person, she extended her kindest favour to us, which was a great honour. Lady Sŏnhŭi met my mother, and in her gentle way immediately made friends with her new in-laws. Mother was so calm, and spoke with everyone, yet so precisely and modestly, that everyone at court praised her and thought highly of her. This is the reason that when mother died in 1755, all the court ladies wept — so much had mother won their hearts.

After three days' stay at the T'ongmyŏng-jŏn Mansion, I returned to the crown prince's palace and settled into the Kwanhŭi-hap pavilion. By this time mother had returned home, leaving me completely desolate. She, on the other hand, had not displayed any emotion, but said farewell calmly, advising me that, as the three royal ladies loved me, and the king treasured me as his own daughter, I should strive out of filial piety to do my best for them, bringing happiness to home and country. 'If you value your parents,' she concluded, 'please keep these words in mind.'

But when she got into the palanquin, she wept and so earnestly entreated the court maids to look after me, that they said 'How can we refuse your request, since we have seen you like this.'

On 27 April 1744 I humbly presented myself at the Sŏnwŏn-jŏn hall, and on the twenty-ninth, at the Royal Ancestral Temple. I was much moved when both the king and Lady Sŏnhŭi showed their pleasure, and praised me for having gone through the national wedding ceremony, wearing such a heavy formal hairstyle, without making any mistake.

My father used to come to court on the first and fifteenth days of the month. But he would only visit me when the king permitted it, and even then would not stay very long, saying 'They are extremely strict at court, and a mere commoner should not stay too long.' But whenever he came, he was full of advice, and would also go to see the crown prince and encourage him to study. He talked earnestly to the prince about classics and history, yet in a way that the prince would understand, and the prince accordingly was very fond of him and treated him especially well.

In November 1744 father passed the major state examination. The crown prince was delighted at the news and came over to my residence. At the time, none of Queen Dowager Inwŏn's family or Queen Chŏngsŏng's family had passed this examination. The members of Queen Chŏngsŏng's family in particular had all failed to make a mark in life. Although the prince was too young to understand all this, he was nevertheless delighted and fascinated.

After the ceremony of presenting a red tablet to the successful examination candidates, father had an audience with the king. The king, who had been very disappointed when father failed the examination the previous year, was very pleased with father's success and presented him with flowers by way of congratulation.

Both queens, Inwŏn and Chŏngsŏng, called me in and praised father, saying that it was a most happy event that the royal father-in-law had passed the state examination. Queen Chŏngsŏng's family had run into trouble arising from factional strife in the bureaucracy. She was very glad that the crown prince had married into a family which supported the Noron[6] faction, because that was where her own allegiance lay, and she now felt almost like a relation. When father passed the higher civil service examination she was so overjoyed that she almost wept with delight. I was most impressed by her behaviour.

Father did all he could to help the crown prince in his studies, copying out significant passages from the classics for him, and commenting on the prince's own composition. Although the prince was offically taught by a royal instructor, he actually learnt more from my father. No other official strove as hard as he to direct the prince into the ways of a gentle and virtuous ruler. But what a sad set of circumstances intervened! When I came as a mere child to the court, I was impressed by the prince's character and by his devotion to his father. He respected and loved the king, and also Queen Chŏngsŏng, as if she were his own mother. His filial piety towards his own mother knew no bounds. Lady Sŏnhŭi was naturally kind and affectionate, but she was also strict. Though she loved her children, she brought them up so strictly that they feared and respected her, as though she were not their mother.

When her son was made crown prince, she treated him with great respect instead of mothering him, instruction always preceding affection. And so her son was terrified of her, and extremely careful in everything concerning her. She treated me also in just the same way. As a daughter-in-law I felt most uncomfortable at being singled out for such treatment. From the moment I came to court, I never dared omit the obligatory morning greetings. I used to greet Queens Inwŏn and Chŏngsŏng every five days, but Lady Sŏnhŭi every three days. Though I saw them so often, I never dared to present myself attired in anything but ceremonial dress, nor to arrive late in the morning, as the court regulations were so strict. I was even unable to sleep properly for fear of being late for this morning greeting.

When I came to court, I brought with me my former wet nurse and a girl attendant named Pongnye. Pongnye had been granted to my father by my great-grandmother as a special favour when he passed the minor state examination. I used to play with her as a child, and spent most of my time in her company. She was bright, quick-witted and very faithful, unlike most people of low birth. My nurse was a simple soul, honest, diligent and loyal. I persuaded them to wake me up early every morning, telling them never to forget, whether in the depths of winter, the heat of summer, or in wet, windy or snowy weather, because it was of great importance. It was thanks to these two that I was never late for the morning greeting.

Later, my nurse attended me at the births of my children and served me well. Perhaps because of this she was blessed with over eighty years of life, and her descendants for generations were paid

15

generous wages in cotton. Pongnye was like a second pair of hands and feet to me and always understood my moods. She shared my fortunes for fifty years, and in 1790, on the birth of King Sunjo, was appointed governess by King Chŏngjo. On that same day she prepared *kaengban*[7] for the nursing mother. Even though she is now seventy, she is still very energetic and serves me as well as ever. Both my nurse and Pongnye served me diligently, and as a result they seem to have enjoyed long years of happiness.

In those days, the court regulations were so strict that there were many hardships other than the early morning greeting, but I was never troubled by them so much. I was probably able to put up with such things because of my old-fashioned upbringing. I had many sisters-in-law, whom I treated with respect, but I never imitated them because of the difference in our positions, and patterned myself rather on Queen Hyosun. Consequently, even though she was very much older than I, we loved each other dearly, and I learnt a great deal from her. Of the princesses, Hwasun was gentle and reverent, and Hwap'yŏng was submissive. Both of them treated me very kindly. Two younger sisters-in-law were about the same age as I, and very dear to the family. They had all the toys you could imagine, but I never enjoyed playing with them, which worried Lady Sŏnhŭi. She would say, 'You want to play with them, but hesitate because of your wish to follow the ways of the court. Do not behave like this. Go and play like the other princesses.' She was at pains to guide my every footstep, and I shall never forget this.

When I came to the court in 1743, the eldest of my younger brothers was five, and the next was three. They were both big boys for their age, and looked like twins. After the wedding mother brought them to court once or twice a year. King Yŏngjo was very fond of them, and used to let them accompany him. Whenever he called the elder boy, he would answer very clearly in a loud voice like a cavalry orderly, which the king thought was very amusing. Later this brother grew up to pass the higher civil service examination in 1748. The king was very pleased, saying, 'That child who used to answer like a cavalry orderly has passed the examination. The president[8] has an outstanding son!'

When this brother read as a Confucian scholar-official, the king would clap his hands and praise him, saying, 'You read very well.' The crown prince doted on him, and whenever my brothers came to court, the prince never let them leave him, but would go about everywhere with them, holding hands. Once when the elder boy came to court at the age of nine, the crown prince had just finished paying homage at the Royal Ancestral Temple, and had taken off his crown. He tried jokingly to put it on my brother's head, but my brother held his head tight with his hands and said, 'A subject should not wear it, sire.' The crown prince was surprised, but did not force him. My poor brother was quite thrown into a sweat by the incident. He was certainly different from children of these days!

According to court regulations, males over ten years of age are not allowed to sleep in the royal palace. One day the crown prince kept on calling the younger brother, but when he reached the front gate, a royal guard apparently said something disrespectful, which upset my brother so much that he refused to come any further. So the prince went out himself to the front gate and brought him in, saying 'How can I expect you to help me, when you stand so firmly by your principles?' The prince then wrote something on a fan and gave it to him. I remember the occasion as if it were only yesterday. This particular brother was especially obedient and gentle, and had a special place in my heart.

Seven years after he had passed the higher civil service examination, father was given an appointment as army commander — an exceptional honour. Many would have attributed this to his royal connections, but Lady Sŏnhŭi told me privately that years ago, when my father, who was then a senior student of *Sŏnggyun'gwan,*[9] had had his first audience with the king, the king had said to her on his return to the palace, 'Today I found a subject who can render me splendid service, and his name is Hong Pong-han.' In view of this, it is obvious that the king took him into government service, not because he was a royal relative, but because he was a man of ability who should not go unrecognized. From then on the king entrusted him with the management of finances, grain and soldiers, as well as other important civil and military affairs. Father did his best to serve the state, both by day and night, sometimes forgetting to eat and sleep, completely neglecting his private affairs and concerning himself only with matters of state. Whenever he saw me, he would say, 'I don't know how I shall every repay the king's favour.'

In the meantime, I had become pregnant, and gave birth to a son, Ŭiso, in 1750 but he had died in the spring of 1752. The king, the two queens and Lady Sŏnhŭi were so grief-stricken that I felt very guilty at having displayed such a dreadful example of impiety.

17

Then in October of the same year, by the blessing of heaven, the future King Chŏngjo was born. I had not expected such a happy outcome, in view of the misfortunes which had previously dogged me. The baby was a handsome child with excellent bone structure. To me he looked like the sun and moon rolled into one, like a dragon on a phoenix. King Yŏngjo was overjoyed at the sight of him, and told me that the child's appearance was altogether so outstanding that it must be a blessing from the divine spirits of the royal ancestors, and an omen of happiness for the state. 'I never expected such a happiness in my declining years!' he joyously exclaimed. He also observed, 'A descendant of Princess Chŏngmyŏng, you became the wife of the crown prince. Your body has been blessed to make this outstanding contribution to the welfare of the state. Please rear the child carefully and dress him plainly, so that you may be sparing with his good fortune.' Naturally, I valued his instructions very highly, and obeyed them as best I could. I had not been able to perform my duty as a mother when my first child was born, for I was then too young, but after the sad loss of that spring, everybody at the palace was doubly delighted at this second happy event.

Mother had come to the court before my confinement, but father was on night duty for about a week before he saw the child. They were both delighted, and congratulated me over and over again. They were most excited at my having produced such a handsome baby, and praised me so much that I could not help feeling happy and proud, which was natural enough, as I was not yet twenty years of age. I felt inspired by a new sense of security.

In the tenth month, 1751, the crown prince had dreamed of a dragon playing with a magic stone, and on awakening, he had felt this to be an unusual omen. So he immediately drew the dragon he had seen in his dream on a strip of white silk and hung it on the wall. He was then only seventeen, and it would have been natural for him to have passed off the dream, however unusual it was. Instead, he said that it was an omen that he would beget a son. It was strange that in some respects he behaved like a man of experience and maturity. His drawing was excellent, and I believed that his unusual dream heralded the birth of a sovereign. Although the prince was a silent man, stern and discreet, he would always smile at the baby, and praised me himself saying 'With such a wonderful son as this, you have no need for any worries.'

A measles' epidemic was raging that year, and one of the

princesses contracted it first. The court physicians asked the crown prince and the royal grandson to move to another residence to avoid the disease. At the time, the baby was less than three weeks old and very difficult to move, but, in obedience to the king's instructions, the crown prince moved to the Yangjŏng-hap pavilion, and we took the royal grandson into the Naksŏn-dang hall. Though the baby was less than three weeks old, he was a big baby and so I was not worried about taking him some distance. We still had not appointed a governess for him, so I left him to the care of one of the old court maids and my own nurse.

By sunset, the crown prince had contracted the disease, along with all the court maids, so there was no one to look after him. Lady Sŏnhŭi came in person to look after her son, and my father too stayed awake all night at the prince's residence. The prince's symptoms were mild, apart from a very high temperature, but father tended him devotedly. When his illness was on the mend, he was constantly asking my father to read to him, and maintained that he felt invigorated after listening to the reading. Although I cannot remember all the books my father read to the prince, one of them was *Chu'u shih piao* (*Ch'ulsap'yo* in Korean) by Chu Ko-liang.[10] Father explained, as he read this book, that from ancient times there had never been two people who understood each other so well as Emperor Chao-lieh of Shu Han and Chu Ko-liang, and that this was why he himself always admired the work. He also recalled various sayings of wise kings and famous subjects of ancient times, presenting them in a story form to which the prince responded remarkably well, although he was ill.

As soon as the prince recovered, I myself went down with the disease, and suffered a serious attack, probably aggravated by the worry about the prince's sickness, coming so soon after my confinement. The baby broke out in a rash at the same time as I. He was then three months old, but fortunately he suffered only a mild attack, and recovered without much trouble. Lady Sŏnhŭi and father were both afraid to tell, in my weakened state, of the baby's sickness and so hid the news from me. I was therefore unaware of the situation until I learned that father had been going backwards and forwards between me and the baby, and had become quite distraught with worry. One night he had collapsed and was unable to get to his feet. When news of his distress and concern came to me, I was most remorseful.

The baby had been fed by one of the wet-nurses, but otherwise the responsibility of caring for him had fallen mostly to father, who was at his wits' end with worry. The measles did not set him back at all, and he could recognize the letters of the alphabet by his first birthday. He was certainly precocious and I think much different to ordinary children.

In the early autumn of 1753 the king had the senior super-intendant of education, Cho Kwan-bin, tortured in his presence, and all the courtiers there were very frightened, but our two year old baby waved his hand and said 'Don't shout.'[11] It was amazing that a two year old could be so intelligent.

At the age of three a royal instructor was assigned to him and he was taught the *Hsiao ching* (*Hyogyŏng* in Korean).[12] His youth put no restraints on his learning. In fact he loved learning so much that it was a pleasure to teach him. Once when King Yŏngjo was lecturing to a group of Confucian scholars who had been summoned to court, he asked his grandson, then aged six, to stand beside him and read the book. He read it so well, in such a clear voice, that the royal instructor, Nam Yu-yong, said 'A child of the immortals has come to read this book.' This pleased the king immensely. I do not think there was ever any child so precocious.

There were so many instances of his youthful devotion to the crown prince, his father, that I can hardly record them all. He was not at all like us mere mortals, but resembled rather a heavenly being. This was the magnificent son I bore when almost a child myself, and later I gave birth to two daughters, Ch'ŏngyŏn in 1754 and Ch'ŏngsŏn in 1756. Ch'ŏngyŏn had a very gentle and generous disposition, and Ch'ŏngsŏn had a beautiful appearance and a gentle heart. I regarded them as my two precious jewels. Everyone respected and envied me.

As to my own family, my father was an earnest man; achieved a great name and shone with prosperity. And also I had many brothers and sisters which made me feel secure. When my mother visited the court, she used to come with my youngest sister and brother. My youngest brother was born in the latter part of my parents' lives and so they loved him especially. Moreover he was loyal, pure-hearted and generous. From childhood he showed a spirit which gave promise that he would make a great name for himself later on. King Chŏngjo was very fond of him and played with him, so I also loved him especially and expected great things of him.

My youngest sister was born after I came to the court, at a time when my parents missed me very much. Most people would take more delight in begetting a boy, but my family missed me so much after I came to the palace that when my youngest sister was born, the whole family was overjoyed and I also was glad just as if I had left part of myself at home with my parents. My sister's nature was as flawless as jade and her behaviour was filial. In spite of my parents' and brothers' excessive love for her, she was never haughty. Whenever she came to the court, both queens and Lady Sŏnhŭi doted on her.

At the royal wedding in T'ongmyŏng-jŏn Mansion court maids from all the palaces held my sister in their arms one after another as if they were enjoying the sight of the moon or lotus blossom. This showed how beautiful her natural disposition was. I loved her deeply not only as a sister but also for what she was in herself. She always stayed near me when she came to court and when she paid a visit to the palace with my mother in 1750 at the age of five, and she heard that I was expecting a baby, said 'The king will be very happy' just like a grown-up. Everyone who heard her was surprised and Queen Hyosun hung a pendant jewel upon her jacket. Later on, when I saw her, she was no longer wearing it, and when I asked the reason, she answered 'Because the lady who gave it to me is not living now, so I did not wear it.'

When she came to see me the autumn after that sad national event of the third month, 1752,[13] she wept to see me, and again broke into tears when she held the hand of the governess who used to look after the baby. She was only seven then and it was strange to see how she could be so precocious. For the happy event of October 1752[14] my mother came to court together with my little sister, who, when she saw the baby said, 'This child looks so big and strong he will never cause my sister any anxiety.' Everyone who was there laughed, but my mother rebuked her instead because her words were not proper for a young child. But I told my mother not to blame her because after all she was right.

At that time, the court was full of continuous happiness and my home was also prosperous with my brothers and sisters all doing better than most. So all the court ladies congratulated me on my good fortune. The crown prince treated my mother extremely well, being very respectful to her, just as if she had not been a commoner. My mother loved and treasured him as few mothers-in law do, and devoted her whole heart to him. When my mother came to court, if there was anything which made the prince upset, my mother would calm him saying, 'Things are not like that.' Then he would soon recover himself. When I had Ch'ŏngyŏn in 1754, my mother stayed in the royal palace for almost fifty days, and all the time the prince treated her so kindly that my mother was very deeply appreciative of his favour.

The crown prince had an excellent natural ability, and his learning made steady progress. His spirit and disposition should have continued to make the same steady progress; but unfortunately he suffered periods of sickness between 1752 and 1753, to my immeasurable anxiety and my parents' deep concern. My mother was so anxious that she prayed at almost every well-known mountain and river. She prayed to heaven so constantly that she could not sleep at night. She did all this not only because I was her daughter, but also because she was so devoted to the state and concerned about its welfare.

Since my brother, Nag-in, was born when my parents were still young, they brought him up very strictly, and so he had an intensive education at an early age. His will and spirit were excellent. His behaviour was outstanding, and when he was fifteen he was already like a grown-up scholar. Everyone in our family held him in great esteem, and the servants treated him with great deference as their lord and master. Since he acted in accordance with adult codes of behaviour, his peers dared not despise him and my grandfather always thought of him as the man of outstanding ability in the family. Nag-in had intended to marry in 1743, but had put it off because of my marriage to the crown prince, so that his wedding was finally held in 1745. His wife was a great-grand-daughter of Prince Yŏyang, and a grand-daughter of a retired government official, which meant that she came from one of the most distinguished families. When she was very young she used to come to the court and the king, queen and queen dowager would take a special interest in her. Now all three were very happy to know that she had married into my family, and they sent a court governess to take part in her marriage procession. Both the queen and the queen dowager called for me and asked all sorts of questions about the wedding, thus demonstrating their goodwill towards their relatives by marriage.

When my sister-in-law came to the palace for the first time after her marriage, I recognized that she was pure and graceful, her spirit exalted and beautiful, her appearance dignified and her conduct in perfect accord with the strict rules of behaviour. When she stood among the other young ladies related to the imperial family, she was like a stork among the chickens, as jade among ordinary stones. She and my brother were a really perfect match — a match made in heaven. So in our family the eldest son and his wife were outstanding, and my parents treasured them more than anything else in the world.

My sister-in-law gave birth to two daughters in quick succession, but for quite a long time was unable to have a son, which made my parents very anxious and impatient. But then you, Su-yŏng, were born in the fourth month, 1755, and your bone structure was so outstanding and you were so handsome even as a baby in swaddling clothes, that your parents loved and treasured you more than immense wealth. They held high hopes for you, as one would for a prize race horse, and wrote to me telling me how lucky they considered themselves. I thought it only natural that their child should be so wonderful and so was very glad for my family. Afterwards, King Yŏngjo saw you and was most favourably impressed. He gave you the name Su-yŏng; the greatest imaginable honour for a baby. The royal grandson also loved you very much. I think no child had so many honours heaped on him as you did.

After you were born, my family seemed to lack nothing. But alas! Mother died in the eighth month, 1755. Of course, it is natural for people to be very sad when they lose their mother. But I felt as if I had been quite abandoned in the world. There was no joy left, and I had no desire to go on living. Father, too, was very sad, not only because he had lost a most intelligent wife, but also because of my grief. I tried to comfort my father and to take reasonable care of myself, but I could not forget my sorrow even for one second.

When mother's death was announced, Lady Sŏnhŭi came to see me in person and comforted me as if she were my own mother. Such affection between mother-in-law and daughter-in-law is rare, even among commoners. I was much moved, and could hardly control my grief. After the funeral, when I went to make my greeting to both the queen dowager and the queen, they held my hands in theirs, and wept for my mother's sad death, and tried to comfort me. In spite of my distress, I was aware of the great honour they bestowed upon me. I had no desire to stay on in this world, but forced myself to do so. King Yŏngjo said that I was lamenting too much, while Queen Chŏngsŏng and Lady Sŏnhŭi both chided me for breaking the state customs with regard to formal wear and observing mourning for too long. This made me even more depressed, because I felt that I could not otherwise fulfil my proper mourning obligations.

The wives of my second and third brothers were second cousins to each other. The wife of my second brother was wise, graceful and obedient, whereas the wife of my third brother was gentle and friendly. My parents were very happy with them, but before long they lost my mother. My second brother was then seventeen, and my third brother only fifteen. They felt as if they had attained adulthood in vain. My youngest brother was only six at the time, the same age my father lost his mother, and he did not seem to appreciate his sad situation. But my young sister was old enough to appreciate it; she behaved like a mourner, pitying her younger brother and looking after him like a grown-up, so that they were a support to each other. My youngest brother was taken care of by my grandmother, and my sister was helped by my sister-in-law, so I had no need to worry about their food and clothing, but when I thought that they had no one to fall back on, and how lonely they must feel, I could not stop thinking of them. Each time my sister wrote to me, the letter would describe how much she missed our mother, and I would shed floods of tears.

In March 1756 my father was sent out as governor of Kwangju, and I felt depressed at his departure. What distressed me even more, was that he took with him my grandmother, whom I thought of as a second mother. In the intercalary ninth month, 1756, I gave birth to Ch'ŏngsŏn, and felt very downcast, remembering how my mother had come to the palace for both my previous confinements. The sorrow occasioned by this memory was so great that I was unable to look after myself properly, and since I had been on a meatless diet for too long, I became totally exhausted. King Yŏngjo was very worried, and ordered my father to get some restorative for me. Thanks to this I recovered safely from my confinement, although I was still very weak from my deep-seated sorrow, and father was very worried about me. That same month my father was appointed the provincial governor of P'yongyang and departed in sorrow. Though disturbed by his private affairs, he hastened to obey the royal commands as best he could.

In the middle of the following winter the crown prince was stricken with smallpox. My father was always concerned over his own lack of ability, so when he heard this news away in that distant province, he remained day and night in a cold room, worrying so much over the news from Seoul, that his beard turned completely white. Fortunately, the crown prince recovered from the smallpox, which was a great blessing. But less than a hundred days after his recovery, Queen Chŏngsŏng died. The prince in his sorrow was a model of filial piety and at the national funeral people were moved to tears by his grief. National affairs were in a state of confusion at this time,[15] and the prince did not fully recover from his illness for a long while.

In the fifth month, 1757, father was posted back to the Seoul government office, and we were overjoyed to see each other again after the separation, but a series of anxieties made us unable to do anything but weep each time we met. King Yŏngjo was in an angry mood towards the end of the year, and father was placed in the awkward situation of feeling obliged, through a sense of loyalty, to remonstrate with the king. This made the king angrier than ever, and father was dismissed from office, so that he was no longer entitled to reside within the city gates. The king's affection towards me had never lessened from the time I had come to court, and even at this very difficult period, his love for me never changed. Then, for the first time, I received a stern reprimand, and stayed in a small back room because I did not know what to do.

After a long while, the king ordered my father to be reappointed to his former position. He also called me in and displayed his usual affection. I was fearful at the time, but felt I could never repay the king's favour to me, even were I to break my body and pulverize my bones.

I had many experiences which I would include here were they the kind of thing one could write about. Our country was unfortunate in losing Queen Dowager Inwŏn a month after Queen Chŏngsŏng's death. I felt immense love for both queens, and had humbly waited upon them. Now I had so many worries, yet was left with no one to rely on. I had wanted to devote my feeble self to Queen Chŏngsŏng, staying near the apartment where she was lying in state before the burial, performing the simple rites at noon and weeping bitterly in the morning and evening. And indeed, for five months I followed this practice. But there was no way to repay the affection Queen Dowager Inwŏn had shown me. Her illness had taken a serious turn in one short month, and coming on top of Queen Chŏngsŏng's sudden death, left me all alone and full of grief. King Yŏngjo served the queen dowager day and night, without bothering to remove his robes or belt, and I felt very worried about him. Whenever I saw him, I was overcome by my sense of emptiness and grief at the queen's death.

As soon as the three years mourning for both queens was over, in 1759, King Yŏngjo married again. At the time, there were all sorts of worries in the palace, which no one spoke about. Lady Sŏnhŭi said to me, 'Since Queen Chŏngsŏng is dead, it is the correct procedure for the state to fix upon a queen, and to hold a state wedding.' She congratulated the king and personally took charge of the preparations of the state wedding. She sincerely rejoiced that court would again be complete: her devotion to the king was really outstanding.

When the crown prince had audience with King Yŏngjo after the state wedding, he conducted himself very carefully and devotedly, demonstrating his innate filial piety and sincerity. Everyone in the palace knew that he used to feel very happy whenever he was able to pay his greetings to the king and queen without making any mistakes. Alas! What was the use of trying to explain the situation to heaven! How sad it all was!

The crown prince was an exceedingly affectionate person, and very fond of all his family. He doted on our eldest son, but according to his strict moral code the princesses were never permitted to compete with their brother, nor his half-brothers to look up to him. He respected his elder sisters, Hwasun and Hwap'yŏng, and sympathized with Hwayŏp, because she, like himself, could not enjoy the king's favour. It was for this reason that he was so distressed at her death. And had the prince been an ordinary man, he could not have failed to be short-tempered with Madame Chŏng,[16] to whom the king was much devoted, and whose influence with the king was indeed much greater than that of the crown prince. Yet the crown prince never failed to show warm affection towards her, which would have been impossible for an ordinary man.

In April 1761, our eldest son entered the palace school, and the coming-of-age ceremony took place at the Kyŏnghŭi Palace. However, neither the crown prince nor myself could attend. Naturally I, as a mother, was sorry about this, but I had another great worry at that time, since father was in great distress, suffering from persistent attacks of vomiting, brought on by the dilemma in which he found himself placed through his overriding concern to repay the favours shown him by the king and at the same time to protect the crown prince who was acting on behalf of the king. Whenever he saw me, he would invoke heaven with clasped hands, praying for the peace of the country. I do not report his sincerity here merely because I am his daughter, for it was demonstrated clearly by heaven itself, and witnessed by the divine spirits of heaven and earth.

That same month, father was appointed junior vice president of the council, since the post was vacant and since, moreover, the king was ill. Although he did not wish to accept the post, he devoted himself earnestly to the task, for he felt he owed so much to the royal favour. He was beset by one anxiety after another, and all the while he was trying his utmost to repay the king's favour. Consequently he always appeared worried and cautious. When he went, as a temporary ritual officer, to the Royal Ancestral Temple to pray for rain, he mentally prayed for the nation to be at peace, raising his eyes to the ancestral tablets of many generations of kings. He enclosed his prayer in a letter to me, and I was much moved by it.

My brother, Nag-in, had passed the minor state examination in 1750, and had come to court, where he met the crown prince, who said, 'Your will and spirit are in harmony with each other.' In 1761 he passed a major state examination and often attended our eldest son, as an official of the institute of the royal grandson. He frequently instructed him, and earned great merit thereby. Whenever he was on night duty at the institute of the royal grandson we used to meet each other, discuss state problems and then try to banish them completely from our minds.

In the winter of 1761 when the royal grandson was ten, a wife was selected for him. My father had been invited to the sixtieth birthday of the mother of the board minister Sòng-ùng, and had seen the future queen as a child. He had told me of her outstanding disposition, so when the crown prince saw the name of Lord Kim Si-mok's daughter on the list of daughters of officials, he was inclined to select her. As she was a girl of great virtue, everyone in the court agreed with him, and the decision was reached without difficulty. It was a heaven-sent match. The crown prince was devoted to his daughter-in-law. Though she was very young when the crown prince died, she was overcome with grief and cherished his memory more and more with the passing of time. She still weeps whenever she speaks of him. Her sorrow arose not only because of the crown prince's love for her, but also because she was very filial.

Immediately after the second selection she went down with smallpox and soon afterwards her future husband contracted the disease. Though the symptoms of both were very mild, it was so close to the third selection that I was very worried. Although our son, too, contracted the smallpox at the end of December 1761, he recovered from it within a few days, fortunately for both our family and the state. King Yŏngjo was greatly relieved after his anxiety for his grandson, and the crown prince too was overjoyed. I remember all this as if it were yesterday. I had inwardly prayed to the gods of earth and heaven that my son should pass through his illness without serious trouble, clasping my hands earnestly together. And all the while my father remained on duty at court, consumed with anxiety. But thanks to the royal ancestors, the royal grandson and his future wife came through their sickness without much trouble. The third selection was held that same month, and on 25 February 1762 the state wedding was held — a most happy event for the whole nation.

But alas! How can I bring myself to speak about the Incident of a certain month of a certain year.[17] In the face of this disaster it seemed as if heaven and earth touched each other and the sun and moon turned pitch black, and I had no desire to remain any longer in this world. I tried to kill myself with a sword, but failed because those around me snatched it away. Then I considered that I could scarcely make my son suffer the agony of being deprived of me at the tender age of eleven, for how could he then fulfil his destiny? And so I continued my miserable existence, enduring the unendurable, and crying to heaven.

Father was sternly rebuked by the king at this time, and retired outside the east gate. He returned to the palace when all hope was lost, and the agonies he endured were something no words can describe. On the day itself, he fainted, and when he regained consciousness he had no desire to go on living. Yet like myself, his one aim was to protect the royal grandson, so he too was unable to follow the crown prince into the other world. Only the spirits know of the torments he suffered for this loyalty. The same night I returned to my own home with the royal grandson. Our grief was so great that it would have moved the heaven and earth. Then King Yŏngjo ordered my father to rescue and protect the royal grandson. Although I was overwhelmed with sorrow, I wept tears of gratitude when I heard the king's decree. I embraced my son and cautioned him to express his gratitude for this royal favour, but I myself was very forlorn. When we returned to the court early one morning, in accordance with the royal decree, my father held my hand in the courtyard and wept, saying, 'May you live long with the royal grandson! May the latter years of your life be immensely happy.'

Since time began there has never been a sorrow such as mine. Lady Sŏnhŭi came to see me, sad and resentful, before they buried her son in the tomb mound. This elderly lady was in such agony, that I suppressed my own sorrow and tried to comfort her, saying, 'Please look after yourself, for the sake of the royal grandson.' After the funeral, she returned to her palace and left me with hardly anyone to rely on.

In the eighth month of this year I had an audience with the king. Despite my inward grief, I wept and said, 'Your Highness conferred a great favour upon myself and my son by sparing our lives!'

King Yŏngjo took my hand and said weeping, 'I hardly imagined that you would take it this way. I found it very hard to make up my mind to see you, but you are very beautiful, and I derive a sense of comfort from your presence.'

These words made me feel even more depressed, and I had no desire to go on living. I replied, 'I hope your Highness will take the royal grandson to the Kyŏnghŭi Palace and bring him up.'

The king asked, 'Do you think he could bear to live apart from you?'

I replied weeping, 'It is a small matter that he should be distressed by leaving me, but it is important that he should learn under the guidance of Your Highness.'

I tried to send the boy away, but no words can describe our feelings at parting. It seemed that nothing in the world would make my son leave me, but in the end he went off weeping, which broke my heart. I endured this misery, and the king's favour for his grandson grew greater every day. He was extremely fond of the royal grandson, and Lady Sŏnhŭi transferred her love from son to grandson, and poured out all her grief-stricken love towards him. She shared the same room with him in order that she would not be ignorant of his conduct, diet and other problems. She would wake him up early in the morning, so that he could study from dawn. When her grandson went out for his study, this seventy-year old lady would get up and see to his breakfast herself. And so, although the royal grandson did not usually eat early breakfast, he would force himself to do so, not wanting to spurn her attentions. No one could imagine Lady Sŏnhŭi's feelings at this time.

Since my son had loved learning from the time he was only four or five years old, I was not worried that he might not study hard, although we lived apart in different palaces. However, he missed me more and more as time passed, and longed for me so much that, although he used to go to bed late at night, having kept the king company, he would get up early in the morning, send me a note by courier and get my answer before he could go to the institute of the royal grandson with his mind at rest. Of course, it is natural for a child to miss its mother, but he was like this the entire three years of our separation, which made him seem strangely precocious.

During those three years, I was often very ill, and my sickness was very persistent. The royal grandson would consult with the royal physician about my illness, and like an adult send the medicines prescribed for me. For a ten-year-old boy to act like this shows that he was naturally filial and extremely diligent. I did not feel like going to the Kyŏnghŭi Palace to celebrate his birthday in the ninth month of that year, but I was compelled to do so by a royal command. At that time my residence was a low-roofed house situated to the south of the Kyŏngch'un-jŏn Mansion. The king gave my house the name, Kahyodang, and wrote the signboard himself saying, 'I wrote this to repay you for your filial heart on this occasion.' I was hardly able to bring myself to accept this; I wept and felt uncomfortable. Father, however, rejoiced, and told me to write the name of the hall on all my family correspondence.

Chapter II

The Imo Incident was an affair such as has never been known in ancient times. This is why, at the beginning of 1776, King Chŏngjo asked his grandfather King Yŏngjo that the record of the Incident be erased from the diary of the royal secretariat. Thus the original documents concerning the Incident disappeared, because King Chŏngjo, through his devotion to his father, was very anxious that the general public should not view the documents without understanding the background of the Incident. But much time has now passed, and there are only a few left who know the facts of the matter. Meanwhile, the story has been distorted by those who seek to profit by dwelling upon the calamities of others, and who seek to dazzle their audience by alleging that King Yŏngjo disposed of the crown prince not because he was sick but because the king believed an unfounded charge. Others said, 'One of the king's subjects advised hime to take a course of action which he himself would never have dreamed of, and so, alas, matters turned out for the worst.'

King Chŏngjo, although very young at the time, had been a witness to the whole Incident, and as he was a very perspicacious child, he should not have been deceived. And yet, probably because of his devotion to his father, he was unable to distinguish truth from falsehood and always drew one particular conclusion from the Incident. Perhaps he was afraid of the facts behind the Incident, thus he did not give due weight to them. This was natural in view of his close relationship with his father and his distressed state of mind.

The situation of Your Highness, King Sunjo, however, is quite different, and it is contrary to feelings of humanity and principle of all creatures in the universe that a descendant should be ignorant of such a major event. Even as a young boy Your Highness wanted to know all about the Incident, but your father, King Chŏngjo, could not bring himself to tell you the details. And who else dared to tell you, or indeed knew the truth in detail? Other than myself, there is no one in the royal palace who knows the truth and can inform you. I have tried to record all the details of the Incident, so that Your Highness will not misunderstand this sorrowful affair, and having shown the record to you, I shall then destroy it. But time has passed, and for various reasons I could not set everything down. My life has been one long series of disasters, and is like a well-frayed cotton thread. However, it is against human nature not to let Your Highness know the truth before I die. Therefore I have re-lived that former agony and made this record, shedding tears of blood, and yet omitting a great number of things, which I could not bring myself to relate, and which in any case would only make the account tedious.

As a daughter-in-law of King Yŏngjo, I owed him constant affection, and his favour at the time of the Incident gave me renewed life. At the same time my true and unbound devotion was to my husband, the crown prince. Therefore if I distort in the slightest the relations between father and son, may God punish me with death. Already there are various stories about the Incident, and all are ungrounded and false. Once you read this record, you will understand the whole affair clearly.

Although King Yŏngjo was unable, from the first, to feel very much affection for the crown prince, he could scarcely be held responsible for what took place later. The crown prince, for his part, possessed a noble, good and generous character, but his sickness was so severe that the fortune of the dynasty hung upon its slightest turn. This being so, the outcome was inevitable, and his son, King Chŏngjo, and myself, his wife, had to endure this greatest of misfortunes. Only our sense of duty kept us alive through such bitter suffering.

Now Your Highness wants to know the details of the Incident. Generally, those people who blamed King Yŏngyo said that the crown prince was not ill and that some subject was guilty. This not only fails to grasp the real facts of the situation, but also places the three kings in a sorry light. If you bear this in mind, I do not think it is at all difficult to distinguish the principles of right and wrong in the Incident.

I made a draft of this record in the spring of 1802, but did not show it to you in advance. I have now finished writing this account, partly because my family has been victimized and partly because I was asked to do so by your mother, Lady Kasun, who thought it only right that the descendant of the crown prince should know the facts. So I have forced myself to write this record, which contains all my inmost thoughts, and to show it to Your Highness. Once again I feel choked by the strength of my emotions, and I can scarcely control myself in order to write. I doubt that there is anyone in the world as unfortunate as I! I am overwhelmed with resentment. (May, 1805).

After the death of Crown Prince Hyojang[1] in 1728, the state was for many years without an heir, which was a constant source of anxiety to King Yŏngjo. But in February 1735, Lady Sŏnhŭi gave birth to Crown Prince Sado. King Yŏngjo, Queen Chŏngsŏng and Queen Dowager Inwŏn were overjoyed by this happy turn of events for the state, and all the people in the land rejoiced. The baby crown prince had an exceedingly fine appearance and an outstanding disposition.

According to the records, within a hundred days of his birth he displayed various extraordinary talents: at four months old he began to walk; at six months to answer King Yŏngjo when he called him; and at seven months he could point to the four cardinal directions. He learned characters at the age of two, and mastered about sixty of them. At the age of three, when offered *tasik* cakes by a court lady, he ate the ones with the characters, 'Long life' and 'Happiness' on them, but pushed aside those with the eight trigrams and would not eat them. The court lady urged him to eat them, but he said 'I can't eat them because they are the eight trigrams.'

Later he asked someone to hold up a book with the portrait of T'ai-hao Fu Hsi,[2] and bowed to it. When he came across the character *ch'i*, meaning 'luxury', while he was learning the thousand character classic, he pointed to his royal costume and said, 'This is luxury.' And again when he was asked to put on the seven-jewelled crown, (gold, silver, lapis, crystal, coral, agate and pearls), which King Yŏngjo had worn as a child, he refused to do so, saying it was luxury.

When he was asked to put on the royal costume which he had

worn on his first birthday celebrations, he refused, saying, 'It is embarrassing to wear such luxurious cloth.'

This was so remarkable in a child of three years, that the court lady tentatively put out the silk and cotton and asked which was luxurious and which was not. The prince said that silk was luxurious and cotton was not.

Once again, in order to test him, she asked him, 'What material would you like me to use to make your royal costume?'

He pointed to the cotton and said, 'I would like this for my costume,' which proved that he was really unusual.

His physical appearance was magnificent; his disposition filial, friendly and clever. Therefore, he could have developed a most virtuous personality, if only his parents had kept him near them and instructed him, loving and guiding him at the same time. But instead, they lived far away from him, so that small errors grew greater with the passage of time, until finally matters reached a pitch which defies description. Alas, it was beyond human power to change the unlucky fate of the prince and the sad destiny of the state.

King Yŏngjo had been so worried about the palace of the crown prince having stood so long vacant, that when the crown prince was born he did not take into account what it meant for a baby to be taken away from its parents. He only rejoiced that the palace of the crown prince would now have a master, and so sent the child from the Chippok-hŏn Side Apartment to the long-empty Chŏsŭng-jŏn Mansion. The baby was placed there in the custody of a governess when only a hundred days old, since the king was extremely anxious to establish him formally at the earliest opportunity.

The Chŏsŭng-jŏn is a big mansion, originally built as the residence of the crown prince. Next to it is the Naksŏndang Hall, where the crown prince goes to attend lectures on the classics and histories of ancient China; the Tŏksŏng-hap Audience Chamber where the king lectured to the *Ch'amch'an'gwan*[3] and the junior officials; the Simin-dang Hall where the crown prince reviews his lessons with the royal tutor; and just outside the Simin-dang Hall, is the *Ch'un'gyebang*.[4] Since all these quarters would belong to the crown prince when he grew older, the king wanted him to be master of the Chŏsŭng-jŏn Mansion like an adult prince.

Since the Chŏsŭng-jŏn Mansion was a long way from the palaces where King Yŏngjo and Lady Sŏnhŭi resided, the latter would visit the young prince every day, whether in the depth of winter or in the heat of midsummer. As others had pointed out, they spent a lot of time with the prince. But how could this be equal to having him live in the same palace with his parents, where they could care for him night and day and instruct him continually? I cannot understand why, when the king had only just been sent this precious son to whom he would eventually entrust the state, he did not put formality aside and have the baby brought up by himself and Lady Sŏnhŭi. Instead, since they lived far away, the crown prince spent more time away from his parents than with them, and those who surrounded him morning and evening were eunuchs and court maids, and what he heard were only the trivia of middle-class lives. This was a basic mistake, sad and worthy of reproach.

In his childhood the crown prince was possessed of extraordinary virtue — his manners were completely in accordance with the dictates of ritual, and his disposition was stern. He was reserved in his speech, so the people respected him as they might an adult king. With these natural endowments and disposition, if only he had stayed close to his parents, and if only his father the king, when he was not busy with state affairs, had sat down beside him and helped him with his reading and learning! And if only his mother Lady Sŏnhŭi, to whom the crown prince's success was the greatest aim in life, had kept his hand in hers, instructing him firmly and affectionately in all sorts of things, so that they understood each other perfectly, rather than leaving the crown prince to himself! It was most unfortunate that from the start they should have kept the young baby in the distant Chŏsŭng-jŏn Mansion.

In the second place, it was unfortunate that the king surrounded the crown prince with those peculiar court maids. I am not now recording woman's gossip, but the true facts of the situation. The Queen Dowager Ŏ had lived in the Chŏsŭng-jŏn Mansion and had died there not long before. Since 1649 Lady Chang had been living in the Ch'wisŏn-dang Hall, at the other side of the Chŏsŭng-jŏn Mansion, and calling down imprecations upon Queen Inhyŏn.[5] It was very strange that King Yŏngjo left his baby son in swaddling clothes in such a desolate place all by himself, and moreover allotted Lady Chang's residence as his palace kitchen, ordering that the crown prince's meals should be prepared there. Three years after the death of Queen Dowager Ŏ, all the court maids who used to serve her had left the palace. When the king established the crown prince in the Chŏsŭng-jŏn Mansion, he recalled these maids, which was fair and proper enough. Yet I cannot understand why he had to recall Governess Ch'oe and all those maids ranking under her, who used to belong to the palace of King Kyŏngjŏng and Queen Ŏ, and make them maids of the crown prince's palace. They must have felt as if King Kyŏngjŏng was still alive, and so they were difficult and unfeeling towards the crown prince.[6] I regret to relate that these seemingly insignificant factors led to serious trouble.

King Yŏngjo had been truly overjoyed at the birth of his son, and loved him intensely up to the age of four or five. He would come and stay with the child at night, and the two were very close. The crown prince, being by nature filial and kind to his brothers and sisters, was full of affection for his parents. Although their residences were far apart, this need not necessarily have led to trouble, for the king loved his son and instructed him as I have described. If it had been an ordinary middle-class father and son relationship, there would not have been the least trace of estrangement between them. But alas, much to the misfortune of the state, the king would unaccountably be roused to anger by the most trivial incidents. After a succession of such incidents, the king gradually began to stay less and less at the crown prince's palace, although he himself could not produce an explanation for his behaviour. The boy was just at that stage when a child needs constant care, both in instructions and admonition. It was only natural that with so little supervision trouble began to occur.

King Yŏngjo was extremely devoted to his daughter, Princess Hwap'yŏng. In 1738, he invited the royal son-in-law, Prince Kŭmsŏng, to the court, and allowed him to play at the crown prince's palace after the selection and before the wedding. He showed special affection to his royal son-in-law because of his deep love for the princess. Now the court ladies at the crown prince's palace were those who had served King Kyŏngjŏng, and the Royal Governess Ch'oe in particular was a very straight-laced person, though not possessed of an evil thought. Though loyal she had a jealous, ingratiating nature. And then there was Governess Han, who was very talented, cunning and envious. Although she was now a court maid in the crown prince's household, how could she be expected to devote herself to King Yŏngjo's concerns, when she had originally been a maid at the court of King Kyŏngjŏng? And then again, the lower ranking maids, ignorant of where their first duty lay, did not respect Lady Sŏnhŭi, for they remembered her as a poor and obscure citizen, and so despised her and spoke to her disrespectfully. Sometimes they even deliberately slighted her, which made Lady Sŏnhŭi most uncomfortable, while even the king sensed what was happening.

Prince Kŭmsŏng came to court on New Year's Day, for the scriptures were being read. However, there was a hold up in the preparations for the ceremony, and the court maids of the crown prince's palace, incensed about the delay, sat together, criticizing the proceedings to each other. Lady Sŏnhŭi was much distressed at this, and King Yŏngjo found the ladies very insolent. Yet he did not punish them, for he was afraid that if he did so while they were staying in his palace, they might in turn reproach his daughter and son-in-law. But he was very put out by what had occurred, so his visits to the crown prince became even less frequent than before, not so much because he did not wish to visit the crown prince, as because he did not like to face the maids there. How frustrating to think that the king had put the crown prince in the custody of these strange maids, and that rather than removing them, he preferred to visit the prince less on account of his hatred towards these maids!

Meanwhile, the crown prince was growing older and liked to play, as is natural for children. It was a time when he needed constant instruction, but Governess Han took advantage of the fact that the king's visits were so infrequent, and said to Governess Ch'oe, 'If everyone stops the child playing and doing as he wishes, he will become deeply frustrated and unhappy. So be strict with him and lead him in the right way, and I will play with him from time to time to give his mind a rest.'

Governess Han was clever with her hands, and used to make scimitars, bows and arrows with wood and paper. She and Governess Ch'oe used to take turns being on duty, so as soon as Governess Ch'oe went off duty, Governess Han allowed the children of the court ladies, who were all ready behind the door, to jump out with all the toy weapons, shouting out like soldiers as they invited the prince to play. Though he had the disposition of a king, the prince was attracted by such things and of course wanted to play. After all, even Mencius' mother had to move house three times.[7] The prince would become quite carried away when he played, but at the same time he worried lest his father the king should come, see him playing, and punish him. Therefore, his child's mind, which used to be so open with his parents, now came to know prevarication. The prince also worried lest his mother should find out, and so was reluctant to have even a maid from his

37

mother's palace come to his own residence. He was endowed with a hero's disposition, so he naturally enjoyed this kind of war game very much, but his play gradually developed in a way which is hard to describe. O, the deceit and wickedness of that Governess Han!

It was not until three or four years later, in 1741, when the crown prince was seven, that King Yŏngjo realized the wickedness of Governess Han and dismissed her, at the same time justly punishing many other maids. If only the king had sent all those maids out of the palace, and then carried out a severe reappraisal of his own attitudes. If only both he and Lady Sŏnhŭi could have stayed near their son, providing him the constant instruction. Then he would have become such a filial prince that he would have been a delight to his father. But, although the king dismissed the Han woman, he retained other maids. And he let his child grow up in a great mansion without the care of a respected elder, and doing just as he pleased. Since his everyday associates were only eunuchs and court maids, how could one expect him to learn much?

In the meantime, though it would have been hard to put one's finger on the core of the growing estrangement between the king and the prince, the latter began to feel afraid of his father; while the father for his part came to suspect that his son might grow up in a way contrary to his hopes and expectations. Moreover, the characters of father and son were utterly different. King Yŏngjo was clever and benevolent, well-informed on all about him, yet prompt in action; whereas the crown prince was reticent of speech and hesitant in action. Though he possessed a noble and virtuous mind, he could never find an immediate answer to even the most ordinary question. He was always slow to reply, and when it was the king who asked the question of him, he was even less capable of making a direct answer, although he would have his own opinion on the subject. He used to wonder how he should answer, which disappointed the king. This was also one of the main reasons for the Imo Incident.

Though born a king's son, his childhood education should have been left to his parents, who should have remained with him constantly, so that parents and child were familiar with each other. Instead, the prince left his parents while he was still a babe in arms, and was taken over by the court ladies. They attended his every need, from tying his coat strings to fastening the ends of his trousers with cords, so that everything was made too easy for him. When he granted the royal lecturer and his colleagues audience at the royal institute of the crown prince, his reading would be loud and clear and he would unfailingly grasp the meaning of each passage, so that those present would speak very highly of him, and his reputation was widespread amongst those outside the court. It was most unfortunate therefore that, through fear and deference, he was so slow to answer his father, so that time after time the king was overcome with disappointment, until at last he was both angry and deeply concerned about his son.

The more this happened, the more the king should have tried to teach his son in person, so that their deep affection for each other could have found a common footing. Instead, the king always kept his son at a distance, hoping that somehow he would grow up all by himself completely in accordance with the king's wishes. Naturally, therefore, trouble developed. The two came to find less and less in common, and whenever they met the king's resentment against his son predominated over his affection for him. The son, for his part, was always fearful of seeing the king, and behaved with great caution, as if the audience was some tremendous ordeal which he had to undergo. This all contributed to the growing barrier between them. Alas, what a sad thing it was!

The Kyŏngmogŭng[8] was appointed crown prince in the third month, 1736; in 1741, at the age of seven, he discussed the Chinese classics; and in the first month, 1742, he paid homage to the Royal Ancestral Temple and later entered the royal institute of the crown prince. Everyone admired his natural disposition. In the third month, 1743, he celebrated his coming-of-age ceremony, and early the following year he was married to me.

When I came to the royal palace and understood the situation there, I felt I could not relax for a single minute, and behaved fearfully and cautiously. There were three royal consorts — the queen dowager, the queen and Lady Sŏnhŭi — and court regulations were so strict and royal etiquette so important, that there was not the slightest regard for persons as individuals. The crown prince himself had an exceptional respect for the court code, but he was quite unsure of himself in the presence of his father. So this ten-year-old child never dared to sit face to face before his own father, and would rather go to the other extreme of prostrating himself before the king like any government official.

He never washed his face or combed his hair down in time for the morning greeting, and so had to do this in a flurry at his reading time. Whenever we went for the morning greeting, I would wash my face early, put on the heavy formal headdress and court costume and wait, anxious to go, but the crown prince was never ready, and I always had to wait for him, for a princess was not supposed to go unless preceded by the prince. Even to my child's mind it seemed strange that the crown prince took such a long time to wash his face, and I thought that something must have been wrong with him.

Sure enough, during 1745, he was not like his usual self as he had been before when playing and bounding fiercely about; there was something unusual about him and he seemed to have fallen sick, though not with any specific disease. The court maids clustered together and whispered about it; they seemed worried. Towards the end of the year he fell seriously ill and began to behave in an unusual manner.[9] Since his sickness was now serious, shamans were consulted. They were all of the opinion that this misfortune resulted from the crown prince's stay in the Chȯsȯng-jȯn Mansion. So we prayed at the ancestral hall and recited numerous incantations, and spent a fortune on exorcism, but the crown prince did not recover. He left the Chȯsȯng-jȯn Mansion and moved into the Yunggyȯng-hȯn Side Apartment, in order to avoid further misfortunes. I moved into the nearby Chippok-hȯn Side Apartment in order to serve him. In the first month, 1746, we moved to the Kyȯngch'un-jȯn Mansion. The crown prince was then twelve years old, and since the Kyȯngch'un-jȯn Mansion was close to both the Yȯngyȯng-dang Hall and Chippok-hȯn Side Apartment, Lady Sȯnhȕi visited us frequently.

Princess Hwap'yȯng had a kind, generous, obedient and frugal nature. She doted on her brother and asked him to stay at the Yȯn'gyȯng-dang Hall, and so they grew very close to one another. Since King Yȯngjo was so devoted to this daughter, he also treated the crown prince very well, associating him with the princess' happiness, and consequently causing the crown prince to be less afraid of his father. If only Princess Hwap'yȯng had lived, she could have helped to improve the relationship between the king and his son!

During 1747, the crown prince studied earnestly, and life was for a time free from problems. But in the fourth month of that year, the long galleries of the Ch'angdȯk Palace were burnt down, and the king moved into the Kyȯnghȕi Palace. The crown prince moved to the Chȕphȕi-dang Hall, but as Lady Sȯnhȕi and Princess Hwap'yȯng were far removed in the Yangdȯk-dang Hall and

Illyŏng-hŏn Side Apartment, the prince could now see his mother and sister only rarely. From that time on, the crown prince started to abandon himself to amusements.

Princess Hwap'yŏng died in the sixth month, 1748. King Yŏngjo's agony at the loss of his daughter, whom he had loved so much more than an ordinary child, was so overwhelming that it threatened to affect his health, and Lady Sŏnhŭi was similarly affected. Both of them were so overcome at losing the princess, that all other matters were driven from their minds, and they could not devote proper attention to their son.

The crown prince, in the meantime, did not hesitate to try his hand at more and more amusements until there was nothing he had not tried: he was well skilled in the techniques of archery and swordsmanship, and concentrated on such a practice. But he also passed the time in drawing, and asked Kim Myŏng-gi, a blind fortune-teller in charge of national prayers, to write down various apocryphal and heterodox works for him. Being fond of such books, he learned them by heart. How could he be expected to be sound in his learning, when his interest was captured by that sort of thing! When the king kept him nearby, he worked hard at his studies and there was no barrier between father and son. But as soon as the prince lived apart from his father, he started to play about again and stopped concentrating on his studies, which set father and son against each other even more. Things would not have reached such a dreadful state if only his parents had kept him under their control. Yet for some incomprehensible reason, the king never sincerely instructed his son, and never sat down together with him when they were alone. Instead he left his son to do just as he pleased, and paid him no attention, yet always scolded him in the presence of others, as if intent on maligning his son.

Once the king was ill, and was visited by Queen Dowager Inwŏn, all the princesses and both royal sons-in-law, Prince Wŏlsŏng and Prince Kŭmsŏng, so that there was a great gathering. Then the king ordered the court maids to bring in all the crown prince's toys and show them to everyone, embarrassing his son in the presence of all these people.

As for the crown prince's studies, the king would invite him to the regular administrative board meeting, or some other gathering of all the government officials, and then question him about the meaning of particular phrases or passages. His questions would be unkind, concentrating on points to which his son could not give a

41

clear reply, so the prince, who was generally hesitant in answering his father even on points about which he was certain, would become panic-stricken and unable to speak before such a large audience. Then the king would scold the crown prince, criticizing him in the presence of the others. When this happened time after time, the crown prince became very upset and angry about the king not instructing him sincerely, although he never dared to blame his father. He became very afraid of his father, and also very antagonistic towards him and, to my utmost grief, lost his filial character.

While Princess Hwap'yŏng was alive, she used to take her brother's part, so that whenever such problems arose, she would remonstrate with the king in favour of her brother. She helped the prince a great deal in this way. But after her death there was no one to intervene with the king whenever he was excessively severe with the prince or otherwise lacking in affection towards him. So the king's affection for the crown prince decreased, while the prince feared his father so much that he could no longer fulfil his duty as a son. If only Princess Hwap'yŏng had been alive, she could have helped to improve both the attitude of the father and the filial piety of the son. The untimely death of that virtuous princess really affected the fate of the kingdom! I still regret it very deeply.

The crown prince had a very generous disposition, and was broadminded and flexible. He was also extremely faithful, and would speak to his subordinates in a way which inspired confidence. Although he was terrified of his father the king, whenever he was questioned about some misdemeanour he always confessed the truth, so that the king knew he was never telling a lie.

The prince's brotherly affection was as commendable as his filial piety. It might be thought natural for him to love Princess Hwap'yŏng most of all, for she was the king's favourite, but this was not because he allowed his feelings to be led by any political consideration. It was purely because he loved her sincerely. He was always sympathetic towards Princess Hwasun, who had grown up without her mother, and he respected her as his eldest sister. As for Princess Hwahyŏp, who was born in 1733, she was exceptionally beautiful and filial, but was never loved by her father the king, probably because of the heartbreak he had suffered at her birth, when he had hoped for a son. So he did not even let her stay in the same palace with Princess Hwap'yŏng; while Princess Hwap'yŏng, disturbed at receiving all the king's love, vainly begged him not to treat her in this way. Even Princess Hwahyŏp's husband, Prince Yongsŏng, was unable to enjoy royal favour, because of the king's attitude to the princess. The crown prince was always very sympathetic towards Princess Hwahyŏp and treated her with great affection, for he was closest in age to her and had likewise failed to gain the affection of his father the king.

The prince was fifteen in 1749, and celebrated his coming-of-age ceremony on 10 March. It was then decided that he should begin full married life on the 15th. Now that the crown prince, son of the king's declining years, was fifteen years old and married in fact as well as in name, it would have been wonderful if the king had been pleased to accept the situation without interference. Instead, the king suddenly ordered the prince to deputize for him: why I could not understand. It was after the crown prince began to deputize for the king, and on the day of coming-of-age ceremony that, to my utmost sorrow, countless troubles began.

King Yŏngjo was filial towards his parents, and held his ancestors in the highest regard; he respected heaven and loved his people. His abundant virtue and sincerity far exceeded that of the greatest kings who had ever lived. I do not think, judging from my own experience and from the historical records, that there was any other king in previous generations who could be compared to him. However, he had experienced many difficulties during his reign, such as the Sinim Disaster[10] and the Musin Rebellion,[11] and he now appeared to have a mental block towards some things, while he fretted and worried over others. It is impossible for me to record all such instances. For example, he used to choose his words very carefully, and shunned such words as 'death' or 'return'. Then again, before coming back to the palace, he would change the robe he had worn for the regular administrative board meeting, or for whatever other activity, outside the royal residence at the palace. After he had had a conversation he considered ominous, or had happened to hear ominous words, he would rinse out his mouth and wash his ears, or call someone to come and speak the first words before he went into the royal residence. He was very particular about which doors he used when setting out on some pleasant mission, distinguishing them from those he used when going out to perform some unpleasant duty. He would never allow anyone he disliked to stay at the residence of someone he loved, and would not even permit someone whom he disliked to go through a place where someone he loved had walked. I regret to say that I cannot respect him for such extremes of love and hatred.

Even before the crown prince began to deputize for him, the king would often ask the crown prince to preside at the torture of a condemned criminal; or to represent him at public matters connected with the board of punishment; or the investigation of a major crime; or some other ominous matter connected with the court.

Before entering the quarters of Princess Hwap'yŏng and Princess Hwawan, who was born in 1738 and was now known as Madame Chŏng, the king would change his robe of audience for a fresh one. On the other hand, when he passed by the crown prince's residence, he would stop outside and without changing the robe which he had worn for outside administrative business, would call the crown prince and ask, 'Have you had your meal?' After hearing the crown prince's reply, he would wash his ears and throw the water into Princess Hwahyŏp's courtyard. However, since this residence was on a higher level, he had to throw it over the wall and usually did not succeed. He would change into a fresh robe before seeing some of his other daughters, whereas after exchanging a few words with his precious son, he would rinse out his mouth before hurrying off. This is why the crown prince used to tell Princess Hwahyŏp jestingly, 'We are part of the paraphernalia for purification!' He was very grateful to Princess Hwap'yŏng, who tried her best to make him comfortable. He always loved and treasured her, and was never suspicious or jealous of her. Everyone in the court admired him for this behaviour. Lady Sŏnhŭi, though saddened about the bias of the king's affection, could do nothing about it.

There were certain public matters, such as those connected with the board of punishment and executions, which the king would never supervise in person. Instead he entrusted eunuchs with these duties, while he remained inside the palace with the princesses. The king explained that his reason for ordering the crown prince to deputize for him was that, since the death of Princess Hwap'yŏng in 1748, he himself was grief-stricken and very often sick and in need of rest. In fact, the reason was that he wished to entrust the crown prince with those affairs which he himself shunned to take into the inner court, or those which he could not entrust to the eunuchs. After the crown prince began acting for the king, the latter administered public affairs with the aid of his eunuchs, and conducted the first three regular administrative board meetings of the month with the crown prince in attendance, while the crown prince conducted the other three regular administrative board meetings.

When the crown prince was acting for the king, there were always difficulties between them, and everything the crown prince did seemed to be wrong. Whenever a court official wrote a memorial to the king, referring to some state problem or criticizing the opposite faction, the crown prince would be unable to reach a decision himself and would report to the king. Then, even if the matter had nothing to do with the crown prince, but concerned one of his subordinates, the king would get angry, saying, 'It is because the crown prince is unable to maintain harmony amongst our subjects that a memorial such as this has been sent. This sort of thing never happened before.' So he would blame the crown prince. If the prince simply reported the memorial to the king, the king would scold him saying, 'As you can't even decide such an easy matter, what is the good of letting you act on my behalf?' If he did not report, the king would again rebuke him, saying, 'How dare you decide such an important issue without referring it to me?'

If the crown prince acted in one way, the king would blame him for not doing the opposite; and if he acted the other way, then the king would again blame him. He would become upset and oppose the crown prince's every effort. What was worse, if the people were suffering from cold and hunger, or there was some natural calamity such as a drought, then the blame was laid at the door of the crown prince's lack of virtue. Consequently, if it became cloudy or a thunderstorm appeared in winter, the crown prince would become very concerned lest the king blame him. He was terrified of everything, suffered from evil thoughts and delusions, and gradually became mentally sick.

King Yŏngjo was very virtuous and benevolent, and usually looked into matters very closely. Yet, to my great grief, he did not realize that his precious crown prince was falling ill. The repeated alarms caused by the king's rebukes, and concern over the king's anger, made the crown prince, who was clever and perspicacious, but was never allowed to follow his judgement in anything, feel very uncomfortable and sad. For example, the king would never ask him to attend splendid spectacles such as the special state examination,[12] or the testing of the skilled archers, or the state military final examination. Instead, he would ask him to be present at the interrogation of condemned criminals. How then could the prince be comfortable and happy?

Perhaps the prince should have tried to demonstrate his continuing filial devotion towards the king, even though his father went too far; or perhaps the father should have been more affectionate towards the son, even though he could not believe in him. But for no particular reason, relations between them worsened indicating, I think, that such was the will of heaven and the fate of the realm, and therefore something which human effort could not avoid. Yet on the other hand, since everything I witnessed is still vivid in my mind, and the agony engraved on my heart, I cannot but record the real state of affairs, even though I feel quite guilty in doing so. The fact is that King Yŏngjo and the crown prince appeared to be lacking in virtue toward each other. I am choked with emotion as I face the writing paper.

Even at the age of fifteen, the crown prince had never been given the opportunity of accompanying the royal procession to the tombs of the previous kings. As he grew older, he very much wanted to see the countryside, so whenever the board of rights suggested to the king that the prince should accompany the royal procession to Seoul or to the royal tombs, he would be in a high state of agitation awaiting the king's decision. But when, time after time, he was denied permission, he felt initially startled and mistreated, but gradually became more and more deeply offended and sometimes even wept.

The crown prince had always been devoted to his parents, but had never been able to reveal his emotions openly. The king never understood his son, and always showed displeasure at his words and manner, being unable to forgive him. This made the prince more and more terrified of his father, until eventually he fell sick. At these times he would relieve his feelings upon the eunuchs and court maids, or even, many times, upon myself.

When I gave birth to Ŭiso in September 1750, King Yŏngjo should have been very happy, but he was still so grief-stricken over Princess Hwap'yŏng's death in childbirth in 1748, that his sorrow overrode his joy at gaining a grandson. Though the king was very proud and happy about my having given birth without difficulty, he felt anew his sorrow about the princess' failure to bear and rear a child. For this reason he could not even say to his son, 'So you have fathered a child already!'

On the other hand, the king always loved me more than I deserved, for which I was deeply grateful. But, because I alone was blessed and praised I always felt uncomfortable and had to behave with great caution. Even so, when I gave birth, the king did not so much as say, 'You have done very well to give birth to a boy without complications.' As I myself did not appreciate the problems of bearing a son, for I was so young, I felt even less easy. However, whereas the king was upset, unhappy and distressed, lamenting anew over the death of the princess, Lady Sŏnhŭi was very proud of me for giving birth to a son, and thought it was a great blessing for the state. She stayed near my delivery room for seven days, nursing me. The king disapproved and said to Lady Sŏnhui, 'You are inhuman to forget the princess and be so happy.' Lady Sŏnhŭi just laughed and deplored the king's bias.

The crown prince was advanced for his years, and rejoiced in adult fashion that he had a son who would later be a firm foundation for the state. He never raised the matter of the king's failure to congratulate us adequately on the baby's birth, but nevertheless felt very sad, saying 'What am I doing having a son when I myself find it so hard making my way in the world?' Hearing this, I felt very upset.

Although what follows is not something I should record, I cannot help but do so. When I was pregnant with Ŭiso, I often saw Princess Hwap'yŏng in my dreams. She would come into my bedroom, sit beside me, and laugh. In my immature way I thought it was because Princess Hwap'yŏng had died in childbirth, and since she appeared so regularly in my dreams, I was concerned about my own well-being, for I understood that the spirit of delivery is merciless. When Ŭiso was born and washed, I found he had a red spot on his shoulder and a blue spot on his stomach. At first I did not pay any special attention to this, but King Yŏngjo was supposed to proceed to Onyang on 11 October 1750, and on the 10th he and Lady Sŏnhŭi came to see us, their faces half happy and half sad. Suddenly, they undid the baby's coat collar and bared his shoulders, discovering the red spot immediately. They seemed to be very moved and really to think that Princess Hwap'yŏng had been reincarnated. From that time on, they treasured the baby just as they had treasured my sister-in-law, Hwap'yŏng. When the child was newly-born, the king had never taken any special precautions towards him, and had come to see the baby in the robe he had worn for his audience with the government officials. But from that day forth, he was most careful about anything he felt might harm the baby, indulging in groundless and obscure superstitions which I could not understand. His behaviour was probably affected by something he had seen in his dreams.

One hundred days after the baby's birth, the king ordered repairs to be made to the Hwan'gyŏng-jŏn Mansion, where he used to give audience to the people, and moved the baby into this palace. As King Yŏngjo loved the baby so much, I implored him to treat the baby's father better. But the fact is that the king loved the baby because he thought it was the reincarnation of Hwap'yŏng and, as its parents, we were treated no better than before — a thing I could not understand. In the fifth month, 1751, when the baby was only ten months old, the king invested him with the title of royal grandson. Although this was motivated by his extreme love for his grandson, I thought he was overdoing things, and when Ŭiso died in the spring of 1752, the king's agony exceeded description.

In January 1752, with the help and influence of heaven and the royal ancestors, I again became pregnant and in the ninth month, 1752, bore another son. This was the future King Chŏngjo. In view of the few blessings I had received up till then, it was an unexpected happiness. When the baby was born, his appearance was impressive, his bone structure outstanding, and he really was the True Man of Taoism,[13] the heaven-sent one. Around the time of the baby's conception, the crown prince had roused from sleep and said, 'I dreamt about a dragon; it must be an omen that I shall beget a noble son.' He had asked me to get a strip of white silk for him, and he had drawn the dragon he had seen in his dream and hung it on the wall. Naturally, there ought to be an unusual omen before the birth of a sage.

After the bitter loss of Ŭiso, King Yŏngjo was delighted to regain a foundation for the state, and said to me, 'Since the royal grandson is so outstanding, he must be a blessing sent by the divine spirits of the royal ancestors. You, a descendant of Princess Chŏngmyŏng, became the crown prince's consort, and your body was blessed so that you were able to make this meritorious contribution to the state.' He also said, 'Please rear the child carefully yet modestly, for in this way you may spin out his happiness.' Naturally, I held these royal instructions in high regard, never forgetting such royal favour and keeping these in mind all the time. The crown prince too was overjoyed, and everyone in the country rejoiced, even more so than before. My parents congratulated me, clapping their hands in joy. Whenever they saw me, they congratulated me on giving birth to the royal grandson. I was very happy and proud to think that at the age of less than twenty, my body had been so blessed that I was able to ensure the happiness of the state, and that my future was secured. I prayed that in my old age I might long be able to enjoy my son's filial devotion.

In November of that same year, there was a measles epidemic and Princess Hwahyŏp was the first victim. The crown prince moved into Yangjŏng-hap Pavilion to avoid the disease. The royal grandson was moved into Naksŏn-dang Hall. He was then less than three weeks old, but I was not worried about him being moved for he was a very strong baby. No governess had yet been appointed for him, so I sent the baby with one of the old court ladies and also my wet nurse to look after him. Before the end of the day, the crown prince had gone down with the measles and by the time he recovered, I in my turn caught it. The baby also caught the disease. My attack was very serious, coming so soon after my confinement, and compounded by worry over the prince's sickness. I knew nothing of the royal grandson's sickness at the time, it was Lady Sŏnhŭi and my father who withheld the news from me, afraid that my concern for the baby might worsen my own condition. Fortunately the royal grandson suffered only a mild attack, but the crown prince continued to have a very high temperature, even after his recovery from the disease, so my father had to look after him, as well as nursing me and protecting the royal grandson. The worry of going backwards and forwards between three sick beds turned both his hair and beard white.

Princess Hwahyŏp died from the measles. The crown prince had always been very sympathetic towards this sister, since their circumstances were similar, and had showed her special brotherly affection. While she was sick, the prince pestered the man servants outside her residence with inquiries about her condition, and when she died his grief knew no bounds — the true sign of his innate goodness.

In January 1753, King Yŏngjo was upset by a memorial criticizing government policy, addressed to him by a censor, Hong Chun-hae. The crown prince prostrated himself at the Sŏnhwa gate, but received a strong rebuke from the king. It was a severe winter, and it snowed while he was awaiting the royal decision on his punishment. He lay prostrated in the snow, covered by snow flakes until people could hardly distinguish him from the snow. Still he did not move, and refused to take any notice even of Queen Dowager Inwŏn's request to get up. He did not rise until the king's exaggerated fury was appeased: it showed what a serious man the crown prince really was.

However, the king had not completely recovered from his anger, and on the 18th January he proceeded to Ch'angŭi Palace and announced to Queen Dowager Inwŏn, 'I am going to abdicate the throne Madam!'

The latter, being hard of hearing, misunderstood him and replied, 'You may.'

King Yŏngjo then declared that he had received permission from the queen dowager, and would indeed abdicate. The crown prince was extremely confused. He composed a letter to the king, and had it copied out by the officials of the royal institute of the crown prince. Later on, this earned him the admiration of these officials.

The king, meanwhile, remained in his old residence, the Ch'angŭi Palace, and would not return to his own palace. Queen Dowager Inwŏn shut herself in a small back room declaring, 'I have committed a sin against the state, because I am hard of hearing and gave the wrong reply!' She wrote to the king asking him to go back to his palace. Meanwhile the crown prince was still awaiting the royal decision on his punishment, prostrating himself on the ice of the courtyard in front of the Sŏnji-gak Audience Chamber in the Simin-dang Hall. Then he went to the Ch'angŭi Palace on foot, and waited for the royal decision about his punishment, once again prostrating himself. He beat his head against the stones, tore his horsehair headband and wounded his forehead until it bled. You can judge from the way that he wounded his royal body, that he was not just pretending to be virtuous, but was doing so out of innate filial piety, loyalty and obedience. The king continued to rebuke him, but since the prince did his duty obediently, his successful handling of the situation was widely discussed.

The king then ordered various officials of the second court rank and above to be exiled to remote places. My father was included in this number, but the decree did not reach him immediately, for he was just outside the city. He and the prince discussed their problems by correspondence, and their many letters reflect their intense anxiety. I collected them all and showed them to the royal grandson when he grew up. He was much moved by my father's intense loyalty, and took the letters with him saying, 'I will keep them and read them.'

After staying for several days at the Ch'angŭi Palace, the king returned to his own palace, reappointed all the officials and permitted them to attend the regular court receptions. My father too came back, and when he saw the crown prince's bruised

King Yŏngjo

Formal dress as worn by the

A Crown Prince's formal attire

Injŏng-jŏn Mansion

Sŏnwŏn-jŏn Hall

Palanquin

Kyŏnghung-gak Audience Chamber

Informal dress of a Queen

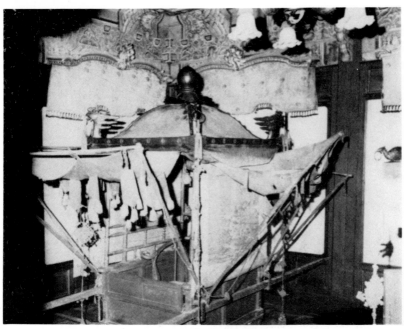

The King's Carriage

Mourner's Staff

Grain Box

forehead, he caressed it, weeping. The crown prince told my father everything that had happened while he was away. I can remember the whole scene as if it were just happening now before my eyes. When not affected by his illness, the prince's personality and filial piety were well-nigh perfect, and he was noble in every way. But, to my amazement and grief, when he was in the grip of that illness, he acted as an entirely different man.

The prince always used to enjoy reading from miscellaneous stories. He once told me, 'People say that if you read and study the *Scripture of the Jade Pivot*,[14] you can raise the spirit of the god of thunder! I shall read this book.' He then took to studying the book at night, so that eventually his mind became troubled, and he had nightmares, declaring that he could see an apparition of the god of thunder. To my great sorrow, all this led directly to a worsening of his mental illness. From about ten years of age, he had begun to suffer from mental disturbances, and ate and behaved in certain ways slightly abnormally.[15] But from the time he began to study the *Scripture of the Jade Pivot*, his disposition changed completely, and he became terrified of certain objects. He no longer dared to look at the two characters for 'jade' or 'pivot', or at the jade pivot charms given him at the May festival to ward off calamity. From this time on he was also terrified generally of the sky, and of the characters for 'thunder' and 'thunderclap'. Indeed, he had always been frightened of the crash of thunder, but never before as much as this. Since he started to study the *Scripture of the Jade Pivot*, whenever there was a thunderstorm he would lie on his stomach with his hands covering his ears, getting up only when the storm was completely over. Neither of his parents knew about this, and I alone knew the seriousness of the situation. These hysterical symptoms began in the winter of 1752, and worsened during the two following years. By that time outbreaks were already occurring very frequently but the problem had now beome part of a permanent mental condition. That *Scripture of the Jade Pivot* is really my enemy!

Meanwhile, during 1753, the prince had an affair with a court lady (*Yangiye*)[16] and fathered a child by her. So terrified was he of a reprimand from the king, that he tried very hard to procure her an abortion. But his effort was of no avail, and she gave birth to a son, In, a queer little thing destined to be a cause of much trouble later. Since the king would rebuke the prince so severely over routine matters his rage on this occasion was so intense that the prince shrank away in great fear. But my father, who thought it unbecoming for the prince to be reprimanded so severely, talked with the king and managed to calm his fury.

In the court, no one is allowed to be jealous. I myself am not of a jealous nature, and from the beginning Lady Sŏnhŭi had warned me saying, 'Do not take any notice of it.' Moreover, I had no need to be jealous of this affair, because the prince did not care for the court lady or even look after her welfare when her delivery time was at hand. His relationship with her was simply a passing fancy, and when she became pregnant the prince was very afraid of a royal reprimand, so he turned his back upon the whole situation. Even Lady Sŏnhŭi was not at all sympathetic about the affair. The court lady's position, therefore, seemed to be very difficult without my intervention.

Uninformed as I was, I did my best to look after her; as a result of which I was severely rebuked by King Yŏngjo, who said, 'You are so determined not to go contrary to the prince's will, that you aren't even jealous of an affair which would upset any normal person!' For the first time since I had come to court, I received a stern reprimand and was quite awe-stricken. It was most peculiar: from ancient times jealousy has been regarded as one of the seven deadly sins, and a woman is believed to have attained the highest virtue when she is not jealous. Yet here I was, criticized just because I was not jealous: it must be my fate! Despite my generous disposition, I would probably not have been so relaxed if the relationship between father and son had been normal and King Yŏngjo and Lady Sŏnhŭi had paid some attention to this baby as a grandchild, or the crown prince had been attracted to the child. But as both King Yŏngjo and Lady Sŏnhŭi pretended not to know about the matter, and the crown prince was so terrified he did not know what to do, any display of jealousy on my part might only have worsened the prince's illness, which was the last thing I wanted.

On 31 August 1754, I gave birth to Ch'ŏngyŏn. King Yŏngjo rejoiced saying, 'For the first time in about a century, a royal grand-daughter has been born. This is a rare occasion.' When Chin, the brother of In, was born the prince was not so severely reprimanded, probably because it was the second time. His malady was taking hold of him more and more, just as water is absorbed into a piece of paper. He went for the morning greeting less and less frequently, and could not keep up with his studies. His mental illness caused him to moan very often, and he seemed to be wasting away with the sickness. So when the king called for an official of the royal institute of the crown prince and in his presence questioned the prince about his learning, the latter was very frightened.

In the second month, 1755, there was a rebellion. The king himself questioned and tortured the traitors at the court until June of that year. The king used to send the crown prince to preside at the execution when the traitors were condemned to death. All government officials attending would be kept standing there according to rank. When the king returned from questioning the traitors, it might be eight o'clock at night or even eleven, or sometimes two or three in the morning, but he never once failed to say, 'Call for the crown prince!' and to ask, 'Have you had your dinner?' He would depart immediately after he heard the crown prince's answer. All this was done just so that the crown prince could be the first to answer a question of the king after the latter had been conducting an interrogation into evil matters, and in order for the king to rid himself of the evil.

In fact, the crown prince was never allowed to attend pleasant and happy functions, but only unpleasant and ominous ones. Even a man who was extremely filial and not sick would be depressed at having to answer, every night without fail, the same question, 'Have you had your dinner? as if the king wished only to wash off the ill savour of his experience. It would have been better if the king had asked anything else, whether it were something worth asking or not. In view of the prince's condition, I used to expect him to fly into a temper and say, 'Why do you call me Sire?' Instead, he would suppress his mental disturbance and answer the same thing each time without fail, even waiting for the king to call upon him. This shows his innate filial piety.

Surprisingly, it was only myself and the children who exerted ourselves to help the prince overcome his illness. The eunuchs and court maids lived in fear of him day and night, and since even his mother was not well-informed about his sickness, it could hardly be expected that the king himself would know the details of it. The prince acted normally whenever he saw the king or any of his subjects, and this made me so sad and frustrated, for I hoped that he would reveal his illness to others, so that everyone, from the king down to the royal instructors, would appreciate the seriousness of his condition, however shocked they might be. I cannot describe how oppressed I felt by these tremendous anxieties concerning the king and crown prince.

About December, Lady Sŏnhŭi was sick and the crown prince went to see her at the Chippok-hŏn Side Apartment. However, King Yŏngjo did not like him staying anywhere near where Princess Hwawan was residing, and flew into a temper saying, 'Go back immediately!' At that command, he jumped out of the window and came hastily home. On the same day the king instructed him most firmly to stay in the Naksŏn-dang Hall, and not go to the Ch'ŏnghwi Gate, but to read the sections on T'ai-chia (*T'aegapp'yŏn* in Korean) in the *Book of the Documents*, together with the commentary.[17] The crown prince was so upset at being treated in this way, when he had simply gone to see his sick mother and had done nothing wrong, that he was on the verge of killing himself. However, he calmed down later. The relationship between father and son was now worse than words can tell.

On New Year's Day, 31 January 1756, the king received an honorary title, but he did not invite the crown prince to attend the ceremony. The prince's condition was deteriorating so much that he now stammered when reading aloud. He used to spend a lot of time in one of the outer kitchens of the Ch'wisŏn-dang, saying it was secluded and quiet. It was this sort of behaviour which always made me worry and fret about him.

Sure enough, in June that year, the king suddenly came to see the crown prince at the Naksŏn-dang Hall, after holding audience at the Sŭngmŭn-dang Hall. He caught the prince looking very untidy: he had not washed himself or brushed his hair, and he was looking so dishevelled that the king suspected he must have been drinking, something which was strictly prohibited. He flew into a rage and shouted, 'Fetch the one who brought the wine!' He questioned the crown prince severely about who had served the wine, but of course no one had, and in fact the prince was not drunk. It was all very strange! Whenever the king felt suspicious about the prince and questioned his behaviour, the prince, as if compelled by fate, would later confirm the king's suspicions. On that day the king sternly questioned the prince, who was standing in the courtyard. Though he never drank wine, the prince was so scared of his father that he could not utter one word in his defence. Taken aback by the king's interrogation, he could not help saying, 'Yes, I had some.'

The king then asked, 'Who gave it to you?'

The prince could point to no one, and just said, 'Hŭijŏng, senior court maid in the outer kitchen did, Sire.'

The king rebuked him bitterly, gesticulating and shouting, 'You behave in such a disorderly manner, getting drunk, when such things are strictly forbidden.'

Then Governess Ch'oe humbly intervened, pleading 'It is really dreadful to say that the prince is drunk, so please smell his breath Your Highness, and find out whether he smells of alcohol or not.' She felt obliged to say this, for she knew that wine was never brought into the court, and the prince could not have drunk any.

But the prince turned on her in front of the king, saying, 'Whether I drank it or not, how dare you contradict me when I have said I did! Please leave us!' Normally he was very hesitant and could not speak coherently in front of the king, but that day he spoke very clearly, probably because he was so unjustly accused. I was pleased that he had answered in this way, though at the time I felt uneasy and fearful.

The king, of course, became even angrier and shouted out, 'How dare you blame the governess in front of me, when you know you should not even scold a dog or a horse in front of your elders!'

The prince fulfilled his duty as a junior very well, by answering very humbly, 'I did so Sire because she ventured to come forth and exculpate me.'

The king eventually exiled Hŭijŏng to a distant place, and ordered the prince to have an audience with the ministers and the officials under them. The instructors of the royal institute of the crown prince were the first to be sent in. That day, the prince was so upset that he became violent enough to have pulled the skies apart. He was very ill, and had never been seen in such a state by outsiders before. When the royal instructors came in, the prince, for the first time, yelled at them, 'None of you have tried to improve relations between my father and myself, and now, when I have been the victim of such unfairness, none of you dare to explain the truth. How dare you come in now?' One of the royal instructors was Wŏn In-sŏn, but I cannot remember the name of the other. He said something to the prince, but did not retire straight away, whereupon the prince became very angry and chased him away, shouting, 'Get out right now!'

Amidst this commotion, the candle-holder which was beside them fell over, touching the south window of a room in the Naksŏn-dang Hall and setting it alight. The fire soon became serious, but no one tried to keep it in check: the prince was chasing the royal instructor out through the gate of the Naksŏn-dang Hall which led to the Tŏksŏng-hap Pavilion. Guests who had an audience with the king at the Sŭngmŭn-dang Hall used to take a roundabout way to the Kŏnyang Gate, passing in front of the Simin-dang Hall, and if the Chiphyŏn Gate were closed, they would pass by the Tŏksŏng-hap Pavilion, where the king discussed the classics with the officials of the royal institute, and then out through the Pohwa Gate. Some such guests were passing in front of the Tŏksŏng-hap Pavilion while the prince was chasing the royal instructor, and the prince yelled at them, 'You don't even try to improve the relationship between father and son by advising the king, but are only concerned about your salaries! Now I suppose you are off to have an audience with the king, you useless bastards!' And he chased them off too. His outburst of anger was incredible!

In the meantime, the fire had become very serious. The royal grandson was then in the Kwanhŭi-hap Pavilion, which was in line with Naksŏn-dang Hall and only about four metres apart from it. I was so flustered by the sudden fire that, even though I was five or six months pregnant with Ch'ŏngsŏn, I jumped from a stone step about one metre high and rushed down to get the baby. I woke up the sleeping baby, sent him to the Kyŏngch'un-jŏn Mansion in the arms of his governess, and thought that we would be unable to save the Kwanhŭi-hap Pavilion. Strangely enough, the fire did not reach the building, which was only a foot away, but turned its course towards the Yangjŏng-hap Pavilion, although the tiled roof of the latter was not even in contact with the Naksŏn-dang Hall. I could not help feeling that the fire changed course because the building sheltered a baby who would eventually be king.

Since the fire was so unexpected, King Yŏngjo thought the prince must have lit it out of malice, and became ten times more furious than before. He summoned all ministers to Hamin-jŏng Pavilion, called in the prince and asked, 'Are you a brigand? How did it happen that you set fire to the palace?'

Once again the prince was so overwhelmed that he could not vindicate himself and explain that it had come about through the candle-holder falling over. Instead, just as in the previous case of the wine, he pretended that he was guilty. I was so angry and upset that I felt as if I was choking, and the prince was so overcome with rage about the unfairness of it all, that he had to resort to restorative pills to calm himself down and raise his spirits. He even tried to drown himself in the well in the front courtyard of the Chŏsŭng-jŏn saying, 'I cannot stand living a moment longer in this world,' It was all extremely frightening and sad. Every effort was made to save the prince, and he finally came out to the Tŏksŏng-hap Pavilion.

In March of that year, my father was appointed the governor of Kwangju and went out to his province. Whenever my father was engaged in provincial service, the prince would feel that he had no one on whom he could rely. Then my father was summoned to have an audience with the king, in connection with the events I have just related. The king, speaking with the deepest concern, told him all that happened while he was away; while the prince talked about the unfairness of both the wine and fire incidents, saying, 'I feel so sad and resentful, that I just don't see how I can live any longer'.

My father seemed to realize the true significance of all this and told the king repeatedly, 'Your Highness, please do not abandon your affection for the Prince,' while he tearfully urged the prince, 'Please try constantly to improve your filial devotion.' Father was generally successful in calming the prince's outraged feelings, and this time was no exception.

I was grief-stricken at losing my mother in the autumn of the same year, at a time when the prince's condition was steadily deteriorating and anxieties came one after another. On top of all this, moreover, I had suffered such unfairness, that I was flustered whenever my father came to court. I remember vividly how we embraced each other and wept. The prince had been so frightened by the earlier confrontation with his father, that his illness worsened and he frequently behaved outrageously in front of his mother. He studied the classics less and less, and restricted his efforts to attending the regular administrative board meetings, and even then displaying no interest in the proceedings. However, such depression was unnatural to him, and when the king was away on royal processions, he used to go to a courtyard at the rear of the palace, and shoot with bow and arrows, or ride a horse. He also practised with various weapons, and played with eunuchs, who even blew trumpets and beat drums for him.

The seventieth birthday of Queen Dowager Inwŏn fell in the seventh month of that same year. A special state examination for those sixty years old and over was held at court, while the king gave audience to all the government officials in the rear courtyard. Strangely enough, the prince was allowed to attend this function, and was overjoyed to get through the audience without any trouble. Judging from this instance, it would seem that the prince's final misfortune need never have come about if the king had felt sympathetic towards him and had treated him calmly and affectionately, so that the prince's abilities were not over-taxed. It seemed as if both father and son could not help behaving in this way — as if it were the heavenly will.

At the age of twenty-two, the prince had still never accompanied the king to the royal tombs, although he had for a long time been anxious to go. He had become increasingly sad and depressed with every lost opportunity. On 27 July 1756, he was allowed for the first time to accompany the king to Myŏngnŭng Royal Tomb, which cheered him considerably. He had purified himself as best he could, and managed his homage at the royal tomb without difficulty. While he was away, he wrote to Queen Dowager Inwŏn, Queen Chŏngsŏng, Lady Sŏnhŭi and even to the children — a letter which I still have in my keeping. On such occasions, he gave no indication of being sick and was just pleased to have completed paying homage without any trouble and to be returning to the palace.

For some time after this visit to the tomb the prince was able to escape any major reprimands because his sister, Madame Chŏng, gave birth to a girl at the end of August, and the king was too happy to bother him. It would have been quite natural for the prince to have resented his sister, since the king loved her so much, while ignoring him. Yet he always treated her in a brotherly way and congratulated her on giving birth without complications. Apparently it was Madame Chŏng who had asked the king to take the prince to the royal tomb with him, having been requested by Lady Sŏnhŭi to obtain the king's permission. Lady Sŏnhŭi had pointed out that even the people would think it strange that the prince had never accompanied the king to the royal tombs, concluding, 'So please advise your father to give permission.'

In the intercalary ninth month of that year, Ch'ŏngsŏn was born. On my previous confinements, the prince had always come with great pleasure to see the new-born child, but this time he stayed away. From this it can be seen how sick he was. Not long afterwards, father was appointed governer of P'yŏngan province and left immediately, despite his anxiety about our steadily worsening situation.

At the end of December the prince contracted smallpox and came out in a rash. Though his symptoms generally were mild, the rash itself was so bad that it caused me serious concern, but it was eventually cured and the prince recovered. It was very fortunate that, despite his raging temperature, the prince recovered so well from the disease. Lady Sŏnhŭi had come and worried over him night and day, while the royal grandson had been sent to Kongmok-hap Pavilion to avoid the contagion. I myself stayed with the prince to nurse him. The room was very narrow; it was bitterly cold and steam had frozen all around the walls. However, the prince survived this serious illness, to the boundless blessing of the state. The king never once came to see his sick son, and as my father was in faraway P'yŏngan province, I alone cared for him, putting all my efforts into the task. After he had rid himself of the spirit of smallpox, the prince came to Kyŏngch'un-jŏn Mansion and recuperated there.

Then on 1 April 1757, Queen Chŏngsŏng's chronic illness suddenly took a turn for the worse. Her hands and feet turned bluish-green, and she vomited a chamberpot full of blood, which was not red but strangely black. Her illness must have building up for many years, perhaps since childhood. It gave me a terrible shock, but I was the first to go and see her. The prince followed soon after. The queen was in a critical condition after losing so much blood, and everyone was moved by the sight of the prince, tears streaming dowm his face, holding the utensil into which Queen Chŏngsŏng had vomited. Before anyone had even had a chance to inform the king, the prince had gone in person to the secretarial office of the queen's palace, accompanied by someone holding the pot, and had tearfully shown it to the court physician. Although the prince had always been treated with the warmest affection by the queen, one might have expected there to have been some reserve in his attitude towards her, since he was not her own child. Yet he acted like this of his own accord, for he was born with a good and filial nature. No one could imagine that he was sick when he behaved like this.

That night Queen Chŏngsŏng kept telling the prince to return to his palace, for she thought the prince should not stay awake at night so soon after recovering from such a serious illness. At last, about one o'clock in the morning, the prince returned to the Kyŏngch'un-jŏn Mansion, but before long, at dawn, a court maid came and said, 'The queen has fallen into a coma and does not respond, however many times we call her.'

The prince was shocked to hear this and went to see her. The queen had indeed fallen into a coma, and lay as if in a deep sleep, nor did she reply to the prince's persistent attempts to address her. Many, many times the prince called to her, saying, 'I have come to see you,' but the queen remained totally unconscious. The prince wept in indescribable agony.

It was the morning of the following day and the king, who had now been informed, came to see the queen. Although relations between the king and the queen were not particularly good, he had come to see her because of the critical state of her illness. The prince, once again, was terrified at the sight of the king, and stopped lamenting over the queen, bowing deferentially without being able to raise his head. The prince had been deeply concerned over the queen's condition, and had wept over her failure to respond to him. He had called her name in such agony that those around him had been moved to tears. If only he had now been able, despite his fear of his father the king, to demonstrate the same sorrow, to assist the king in feeding ginseng tea to the queen, and explain to him the symptoms of her illness! But instead, he threw himself down on his knees in fear in the midst of all the flurry and commotion in that small room. Naturally, the king was unaware that the prince had been overcome with tears only a short while before. He criticized the prince for the way he wore his royal robes, even for the way he wrapped his legs in puttees, saying, 'How dare you behave like this when the queen's condition is so critical!' I felt choked with the emotion, knowing the devotion that lay hidden beneath the prince's exterior, yet I could hardly say that he had not been like this a moment before. The king simply thought that the prince was not devoted to his parents, and was behaving very impolitely. Lady Sŏnhŭi and I were most distressed about the incident.

Unfortunately the royal son-in-law, Prince Ilsŏng, was critically ill at the same time, and Princess Hwawan was sent back to him. The king was extremely worried, and more distracted than words can express. In the meantime the queen's condition deteriorated and she died at about four o'clock in the afternoon of 3 April 1757. The crown prince came to announce the death at the outer chamber of the Kwalli-hap Pavilion. I, too, was going to announce the death, invoking the spirit of the deceased, but just then the king was telling a number of court ladies how he had seen the queen and how she had died. He talked at such length until it was getting dark. The crown prince, unable to announce the death until it was very late, was extremely distressed, and beat his breast with his hand. Then news of the death of the royal son-in-law, Prince Ilsŏng, reached the court and the king was so grief-stricken that he wept bitterly and went in procession out of his palace. It was most unfortunate that the announcement of the queen's death — an event which took place at about four o'clock — was not made until after dark.

Thus it was not until the day after the king's return to the palace that the queen's body was washed and clothed. The crown prince rolled about the floor, kicking his legs and calling upon heaven, and every now and then looking over at the queen's body, weeping bitterly and shedding floods of tears. Even her own son would not have lamented more than this! The king might have been moved if he had seen such sorrow, but when the king returned to the palace, the prince once again prostrated himself, and the king did not see him weeping. This made me feel very depressed.

Queen Chŏngsŏng used as her living-quarters a room at the Taejo-jŏn Mansion, but normally slept in a room opposite, particularly when she had a minor illness such as a cold. So, when her sickness became critical, she had herself hastily moved to the Kwalli-hap Pavilion, the west wing of the main palace, saying, 'How could I presume to end my days at such an important place as the Taejo-jŏn Mansion?' And there she died. After her body had been washed and clothed in a shroud, it was moved to the Kyŏnghung-gak Audience Chamber, and placed in a coffin to await the funeral. The crown prince was allocated the Okhwa-dang Hall as a mourner's hut for five months, and every morning and evening before the funeral he attended every ritual after the morning and evening offerings and on some days he carried out the cermonial wailing six times while I stayed in Yun'gyŏng-hŏn Side Apartment in front of the Kwalli-hap Pavilion.

Queen Dowager Inwŏn was then over seventy and very weak. After the state funeral she would lament the death of Queen Chŏngsŏng, but she did not really seem to understand what had happened, and seemed rather bemused. In the middle of April 1757, her condition suddenly grew worse and, though at times it looked as if she might recover, she took to her bed in the secretarial rooms of the queen dowager's palace and died there on 13 May. Everyone was grief-stricken and King Yŏngjo, who was now a sexagenarian, sick and in his declining years, when faced by this great calamity was completely overwhelmed by his grief.

Queen Dowager Inwŏn was a woman of outstanding virtue: it was at her suggestion that the court regulations were made so strict. She had a deep and sincere affection for the crown prince, and from the time I came to court was so affectionate towards me that it is impossible to record all the favours she had shown me. She devoted herself wholeheartedly to the interests of the crown prince, very often preparing with her own hands rare side-dishes to be sent to us — for Queen Inwón's palace had the reputation for serving the rarest and the most delicious dishes in the whole court. She was very worried at the news of the increasing tensions between the king and the prince, and used to say to me each time she saw me, 'Isn't it very sad?' Whenever she saw the crown prince in mourning robes she would fret and exclaim, 'I can't help crying, seeing him dressed like that.'

She laid down a very strict rule in the court that the daughters of concubines should not sit together in a small room with the wives of princes. Although we lived in the same palace, Princess Hwayu alone followed me everywhere, as Princess Hwasun was an invalid. Once she accompanied me into the small room where Queen Dowager Inwón lay sick. The queen dowager was so incensed by this that she exclaimed, 'How dare you sit alongside the prince's wife! Don't you realize her rank?' I could not help admiring the firmness and authority she displayed, even in the midst of her serious illness.

Queen Chóngsóng used to feel very resentful about the king's maltreatment of the prince, and whenever she heard of the prince's eccentric behaviour she would start worrying about the effect on the state, and would often go to talk things over with Lady Sónhúi. When both queen and queen dowager followed one another quickly to the grave the court seemed vast and empty, and the strict regulations were suddenly abandoned. The prince owed so much to the favour of the two queens, that he mourned them both very deeply. If only the relations between father and son had been normal, things might have been much better.

The queen dowager's body was washed and clothed in the Yóngmo-dang Hall, taken to the Kyóngbok-chón Mansion, and laid in state in the T'ongmyóng-jón Mansion until the funeral. On 17 May the body was placed in a coffin, the white top panel of which was covered with a white silk wrap, and borne by palace eunuchs out through the Yóso Gate, which the queen had used when she went to the rear apartments of the palace. The funeral looked like a wedding procession, and I was so moved that I could not watch. The king was allocated the Ch'ewón-hap Pavilion as a mourner's hut. King Yóngjo had been very worried throughout the queen dowager's sickness, and had served her sincerely. For the five months before they buried her he did not once fail to make the offerings of wine and fruit, and to mourn six times a day. He was then sixty-four years old, and the single-minded determination with which he applied himself to his duties was amazing. Yet he felt that, while he himself was behaving appropriately, his son was wicked and behaving wrongly, for he did not know the prince's inner sincerity. Consequently, in the absence of both queen and queen dowager, matters worsened and my hopes grew dim.

This worsening of relations between father and son can be linked to the death of Lady Hyŏnbin[18] around New Year 1752. King Yŏngjo was extremely distressed at losing his most devoted daughter-in-law, and came in person to the palace where she had died to make sure that everything was properly attended to. While there, he met a court lady, the woman Mun. He had relations with her and made her pregnant. While the king continued to pay special favour to her, he also favoured her brother, Mun Sŏng-guk, a member of the royal bodyguard. The lady gave birth to a princess in April 1753. Most people were very concerned about the affair, and it was rumoured that, in the event of the lady not giving birth to a prince, the brother and sister would pretend that she had born a son, and produce somebody else's child. All sorts of strange rumours were abroad, and some even said that the lady's mother was a former Buddhist nun who had returned to secular life and who came to court for her daughter's confinement. Mun Sŏng-guk was a malicious and utterly wicked fellow, who plotted against the crown prince out of the depravity of his heart. The king showed special affection to both the brother and sister, promoting Mun Sŏng-guk to the royal bodyguard and spending all his nights with the woman Mun. The king installed her in the Kosŏ-hŏn Side Apartment, situated below the Kŏngguk-tang Hall. King Yŏngjo had spent his childhood in the Kŏngguk-tang Hall and had later bestowed the hall on the Crown Prince Hyojang. Lady Hyŏnbin had lived there until her death in 1752.

It was in the Kosŏ-hŏn Side Apartment that the woman Mun gave birth to her first child, and to another princess in 1754. The king appointed Chŏn Sŏng-hae as court secretary to this woman, with his office in the rear yard outside the courtyard gate. It was there that the king used to meet Mun Sŏng-guk, and the latter naturally exploited this opportunity. Knowing the difficulties between the king and the prince, he would report every single thing the prince had done, agreeing with the king's hostile opinion of his son. While no one else had dared to report the prince's actions to the king, this Sŏng-guk, relying on his powerful position, and helped by the fact that he was on good terms with all the workmen in the court, was able to hear every detail of the prince's behaviour and to report it fearlessly to the king. The woman Mun also informed him of everything she heard inside the court. Therefore the king, who had been very suspicious of the prince even when he had not known many details of his behaviour, almost choked to hear these things every day. It was most unfortunate for the state and for everyone that this malicious man and woman appeared on the scene.

Although I was aware that both brother and sister informed the king of everything they heard about the prince, I never knew exactly what they had reported. Around 1756, I was in need of some maids, and tried to appoint the daughters of a workman and of a royal bodyguard from the prince's palace. This was not the prince's idea, but my own choice, since I needed someone to help me. One morning I chose the daughter of the workman Kim Wan-su and the daughter of the deputy supervisor of workmen. By noon, the king was already informed of this, and called for the prince, rebuking him a great deal and saying, 'How dare you choose court maids without letting me know!' I was shocked to hear this. Kim Wan-su was a very close friend of Mun Sŏng-guk, and had probably asked him to intervene so that his daughter should not be selected, for he did not want to send his daughter off to court. It was obvious that Sŏng-guk must have informed the king of the affair.

The death of the two queens, coming so soon after the prince's own bout of smallpox, shocked him so much that his mind became affected, and so his illness and eccentric behaviour grew steadily worse. Sŏng-guk, meanwhile, continued to inform the king of every single incident he discovered, and worsened the relations between father and son. While the king was staying in his mourner's hut, he would stop by the prince's mourner's hut, the Okhwa-dang Hall, on his way to the Kyŏnghung-gak Audience Chamber. He would mourn the late queen, but would also rebuke the prince, finding fault with everything in the hut. Whenever the prince went to the T'ŏngmyong-jŏn Mansion he was constantly criticized, which caused his anger to flare up like a fire. The king would always criticize the prince's faults before a crowd of people or when a great number of court servants were gathered together.

In the extreme midsummer heat the king would constantly rebuke the prince at the T'ongmyŏng-jon Mansion, in the presence of many court servants from the palace of the late Queen Dowager Inwŏn, and the prince's pent-up hostility could no longer be contained. From this time he took to beating the eunuchs more and more. Compared to the prince's lofty behaviour and lamentations at the beginning of the mourning period, such excesses, especially while in mourning, were most deplorable.

The prince's obsession about wearing court costume started in 1757, though this is something which I find impossible to describe. The prince had gone through a difficult time in the preceding five months, and in the sixth month when they buried Queen Chŏngsŏng on the mountain the prince lamented just as he had done at the beginning of the mourning period. He followed the state funeral bier outside the city, wailing and lamenting so sorrowfully that all the government officials and the people of the country were moved to tears. This was how he behaved when in his right mind, but the king never understood this. When the prince returned from the funeral and went forward to receive the ancestral tablet there was some trouble which I cannot now recollect. At the time the country was in the grip of a drought, and the king rebuked the prince so strongly that, overcome with anger, the prince decided to kill himself. The sight of him wailing at the courtyard of the Tŏksŏng-hap Pavilion and looking up at the Hwinyŏng-jŏn Shrine was something far too touching for me to describe.

After the funeral the prince became more and more deranged, and started to kill people. First he murdered the eunuch on duty, Kim Han-ch'ae, and brought his head impaled on a stick to show the court ladies. I was completely horrified to see for the first time in my life the head of a murdered human being. It seemed that killing people appeased the prince's anger. After that first occasion a great number of court maids became his victims. I was so overcome that I asked Lady Sŏnhŭi, 'What should I do, for he is behaving like this and his illness is getting worse?' Lady Sŏnhŭi was so shocked to hear what had been going on, that she retired to bed without eating, and worried over the matter. She was going to intervene, but I deterred her, saying, 'I had to tell you all this, for I felt as if I was choking, trying to keep this terrible knowledge to myself. But if you carry out your intention, and the prince finds out who told you about him, he will never forgive me, and I don't know what to do.' How can I set it all down here, and describe how I exerted myself more and more with nothing to show for it? I too wished to put an end to myself and thereby to forget everything.

Queen Dowager Inwŏn's burial took place in the seventh month during a downpour of rain, which enhanced the king's filial piety in following her to the royal tomb and then returning with her ancestral tablet. The prince too was filial, but his illness was becoming more and more serious every day and ever since he had started to kill people at random almost everyone close to him was completely terrified. It really was an incredible state of affairs.

Father returned to court from Kwansŏ in the fifth month of the year (1757), and the king was delighted to see him, relating to him the sad state of affairs at court. Father also met the prince, who was then very sick as a result of the recent distress and tragedies he had experienced. Father and I held each other's hands and wept, overcome by worry and terror.

In the ninth month of the year the prince brought to his palace Ping-ae, a seamstress from Queen Dowager Inwŏn's residence and who was later to become the mother of Hyŏn-ju. He had had his eye on her for many years, and now, having nothing with which to occupy himself and becoming increasingly irritable, he set this lady up in his palace, in apartments which he had personally arranged and extravagantly furnished. He seemed to suppose that, since Queen Dowager Inwŏn was dead, no one would inform the king. Prior to this he had had relations with various court ladies, and if they did not give in to his demands, he would become violent and rape them. He had had such relations with many girls, but did not seem serious about any of them. It seemed for him a means of only passing the time, and he paid no attention even to the court lady, Yangjye, who gave birth to his child. Yet he made a great fuss over this new woman, who was very malicious.

The crown prince had very little money of his own and started spending palace treasury funds, which was really embarrassing. Although the treasury officials did not inform the king, he inevitably found out the truth, probably through the offices of Mun Sŏng-guk. The prince had established Ping-ae in his palace in the ninth month, 1757, but it was not until 21 December that the king found out. He called the prince in and rebuked him furiously time and again saying, 'How dare you do such a thing!' You can imagine how severely the king rebuked the prince on that occasion, since he was wont to blame him continually even when he had done nothing particularly wrong. The king's rage reached such a pitch that he demanded the court lady in question be brought in front of him. However, the prince was so captivated with her, that he forced her, at the risk of her life, not to go to the king. The king insisted that she be brought before him, but still the prince would not send her, threatening to kill her if she went to the king. The situation was critical, but then, since the king did not know her by sight, the prince took one of the young seamstresses to the king, saying 'Here is Ping-ae, Sire.'

The king had always loved me, especially since my marriage, and even when he was displeased with his son he had never involved me or my children in his hatred, as might have been expected. Rather, he treasured us as if we had not been the wife and children of that hated son, and for this I was very grateful. But I was terribly worried about the repercussions of this affair. I cannot adequately describe my anxiety here. For the first time in the fourteen years I had served him, the king rebuked me sternly, saying, 'You must have known that the prince had brought Ping-ae to the palace, and yet you did not tell me. How is it that even you deceive me? I know you love your husband so much that you were never jealous, even during his affair with Yangjye, and that moreover you looked after their child — something I considered a superhuman effort. I felt very sorry for you then, but you still did not tell me, even when he brought in this court lady from the queen dowager's palace, and you do not answer my questions immediately even now when I am in full knowledge of the matter. I never imagined you would behave like this.'

He continued to rebuke me, stamping the ground in rage, so, although I felt flustered and terrified, I replied, 'How could I dare report to Your Highness what my husband did? That is not the way a wife should behave.' To my great chagrin, this answer caused the king to rebuke me more than ever. He had always loved me, and this was the first time I had ever been reprimanded so severely.

Meanwhile, Lady Ping-ae had been hidden at Madame Chŏng's house. Madame Chŏng lived outside the court, and was asked to hide the girl there. That night the king called the prince to his mourning hut, the Kongmok-hap Pavilion, and rebuked him so severely that the prince in great distress went and threw himself into the Yangjŏng-hap Pavilion well. The sight was too much for me to bear. Fortunately the well was full of ice and contained very little water, and so the hut guard, Pak Se-gun, retrieved him without much trouble. However, the prince was so distressed, in addition to which he had done himself considerable injury, that matters deteriorated to a state for which I can hardly find words to describe.

The king, who was already very upset, became even more infuriated by the prince's insane behaviour in falling into the well. Moreover, all the ministers and government officials had been on their way to have an audience with the king and had witnessed the sight. The president of the council at that time was Kim Sang-no, an evil and vicious man who tried to curry favour with both the king and the prince. Father, prompted by his deep loyalty towards the king and his equal concern for the country, spoke out without considering his own position; 'An old saying has it that a subject is very anxious if he is unable to obtain royal favour. Moreover, royal favour is much more to be expected when it coincides with the natural relationship between father and son. The prince has become like this because of the ordeals he has undergone. I would wish Your Highness to reflect on the matter.'

Father and the king had always been in rare accord, and father had never been questioned about anything he had done. On this occasion, however, the king was infuriated by what he said and this, compounded by his dissatisfaction with my earlier answer about my wifely duties, caused him to dismiss father from his government office.

In fear of his life, father hurried out of the city and stayed in Wölkwagye. The people were dismayed, for they had relied on father's good sense in the midst of the violent actions committed by both king and prince. I myself, having for the first time been so severely rebuked, stayed in immense fear in a small back room. After a long while, the king forgave father, re-appointed him and called me in, showing me his usual affection. Though I was distraught and terrified at the time, this extreme royal favour would never be repaid to me, even were I to pulverize my bones and break my body.

Chapter III

At the beginning of 1758 the king was ill, but the prince was unable to go and see him, being ill himself. This created an extremely difficult situation, and I felt quite faint whenever I saw the king. It is impossible for me to describe how hard it was to go on living from one day to the next.

In the first month of the same year Prince Wŏlsŏng died. Princess Hwasun, who had no child, demonstrated her loyalty to her husband by starving herself, and thereby brought about her own demise seventeen days after his death. Although such an act of devotion increased the esteem in which the royal family was held, the king himself was furious, declaring that it was an act of impiety on the part of the princess to die leaving her aged father behind and going against his advice. He therefore refused to allow the erection of a vermilion gate[1] in her honour. I was most impressed that the prince was able to admire her virtuous behaviour at a time when he himself was very ill.

Following the incident of December 1757, the prince had stayed in the Kwanhŭi-hap Pavilion. In the second month, the king was once more upset about something and went to see the prince, and was amazed to find him very untidily dressed. The king came to the Sŭngmun-dang Hall and summoned the prince there, and so they met for the first time since the incident. The king chided the prince about various matters, and questioned him about the reported killings. The king seemed to know all the facts and to be testing the prince whether he would confess the truth. Presumably because of his basic honesty, the prince would confess the truth although he knew that to do so would lead to great trouble.

On that particular day he replied to one of the questions, 'It relieves my pent-up anger, Sire, to kill people or animals when I am feeling depressed or on edge.'

The king asked, 'Why is that so?'

'Because I am hurt,' answered the prince.

'Why are you hurt?' the king asked.

'I am hurt because you do not love me and also, alas, I am terrified of you because you constantly rebuke me, Sire.'

Thus he went on to confess the exact number of those he had killed, describing everything in detail. The king seemed to experience a fleeting moment of fatherly compassion for his son. He calmed down somewhat and said, 'I will act differently in future.'

He then came to see me at the Kyŏngch'un-jŏn Mansion and said, 'Since my behaviour has led the prince to act like this, I shall behave differently in future. Do you think things will be all right now?'

This was the first time the king had referred to his relationship with his son in such a way. I was overjoyed by the sudden and unexpected change of attitude, and replied weeping, 'Of course things will be all right, Your Highness. The prince has suffered constant upset, ever since childhood, because of his repeated inability to obtain your favour. This is what led to his mental illness and changed him into what he is now, Sire.'

The king said, 'The Prince told me that it happened because he was hurt.'

I replied, 'Yes, he has been deeply wounded, but if Your Highness loved him he would recover.'

The king answered, with a pleased expression, 'Then tell him that I do love him, and that I have enquired how he sleeps and eats.'

This all took place on 4th April 1758. When I had first seen the king going to the Kwanhi-hap Pavilion, my courage had melted away, thinking that some awful thing was going to happen. I had been in an agony of anxiety, but when I heard the king's unexpected words, I was moved to tears and said, smiling, 'How wonderful it would be if you could bring him back to his right mind in this way.' I then bowed my head and prayed with clasped hands.

However, the king seemed suddenly to feel disgusted at my behaviour, changed his expression, and went off saying, 'I will do so.'

I could not understand clearly what he meant — perhaps it had all been a dream — but the prince asked me to come and see him. I went to him and said, 'Why did you tell the king about things which he wasn't even asking about? I feel quite dismayed. And you are bound to blame someone else later for telling His Majesty.'

He replied, 'Because the king asked me about things of which he already knew.'

I asked, 'What did he say?'

He answered, 'He told me not to do so any more.'

I asked again, 'Since you had this talk with the king, do you think relations between you and your father might improve?'

At this, the prince completely lost control of himself and shouted, 'Do you believe what the king said simply because you are a favourite daughter-in-law? He is just pretending to be kind. That is why I cannot believe him; and eventually I shall be put to death.'

He did not look at all sick as he said this. Earlier, I had been moved to tears by the passing kindness of the king's words. Now I wept to hear the prince's opinion, always perceptive even in the midst of his mental affliction. For heaven had created relations between father and son such that, even if the king tried not to hate his son, it was as if someone were forcing him to do so; while the son, whenever he met his father, was incapable of prevarication, and was compelled by his basic honesty to confess all his misdeeds. The prince would never have done such things if the king had treated him in anything approaching a normal way. Why did heaven choose our country to be the setting for this strange tragedy?

All this time, alas, the prince's obsession with dressing was getting worse — and obsession is probably not a strong enough word. For example, when he wanted to choose an outfit, we had to prepare ten, twenty or even thirty sets of clothes; and then he might sometimes burn clothes as an offering to a spirit figure which he had erected, before he finally succeeded in making a choice of an outfit. If his valet made even the slightest error while helping him to get dressed, he would feel unable to wear that outfit, and would become very agitated, so that eventually someone would suffer for it. What a terrible illness! As they had to prepare so many outfits, even cotton cloth was scarce in the prince's household. If his costumes were not prepared in time, or the material not procured on time, the life of those responsible hung on a thread. Consequently, I myself went to great efforts to get everything ready in time.

My father came to hear about this and worried not only about the prince, but also about the strain I was undergoing, and the ordeals of all those around the prince. He therefore supplied the material for the royal robes himself. This illness persisted for six or seven years, with many ups and downs along the way. After the torment of selecting a robe, the prince would become somewhat calmer once, with the favour of heaven, he had at last managed to attire himself in it to his satisfaction. The relief was such that he would often wear that particular robe till it got dirty. What a strange disease it was! Among the hundreds and thousands of diseases recorded from ancient times, there was no description of an affliction such as this. Why then did such a precious prince have to fall victim to such a disease? I never discovered the reason, though I cried to heaven for an answer.

After the first anniversary of the deaths of Queen Chŏngsŏng and Queen Dowager Inwŏn, we spent two months comparatively free of serious trouble. The king was obliged to permit the prince to accompany him to Hongnŭng Royal Tomb, in order for him to pay his homage. That year there was a long and tiresome rainy season, and then on the day of the king's procession to the royal tomb it rained so heavily that the king claimed that heaven was showing its displeasure at his having brought the prince with him. Accordingly, before they reached the royal tomb, he ordered the prince to return, and only the king's palanquin advanced. So the prince was unable to fulfil his intention of paying homage to the royal tomb — something which must have distressed all the government officials, soldiers and civilians.

I was sitting with Lady Sŏnhŭi when I heard this extraordinary piece of news. I was quite stunned, as well as very anxious and flustered, imagining how the prince would flare up when he reached home. You can visualize how he felt when he had to come home in such heavy rain, after going out in vain! He was so inflamed with rage that he could not come straight home. Instead he stopped at the capital garrison, and came home only after he had subdued his anger. By then he was so utterly depressed that he looked dreadful. I felt that anyone would be similarly saddened, unless he were sick or were the great Shun himself, famous for his filial devotion.[2] Lady Sŏnhŭi and I took each other by the hands and wept. The prince himself declared, 'There is no way I can go on living now.' Later, to my distress, he thought that it all happened because he had worn his royal robe wrongly. After that incident, his clothes phobia intensified.

In January 1759, the king fell so seriously ill that he could not personally take part in the rites at the ancestral shrines for the first day of the New Year. I was very worried about the prince's going to ask after the king's health. Even if he went to see his father, the king would not be able to look upon his son without rebuking him, and moreover the prince himself was very sick, and looking quite dreadful, so that he did not want to go and see the king. The king felt very sad and hopeless while he was sick.

The president of the council at that time was Kim Sang-no. He used to appear sympathetic towards the prince's unavoidable difficulties, and his treacherous talk gratified the prince. The prince therefore named him as one of those who had helped him since the incident of December 1757. Now, while the king was so ill and worried about being unable to attend to state business, no one knew exactly where they stood, due to the strange relations between father and son. No one wanted to be in a position of conveying messages between the king and the prince, but Kim- Sang-no would talk smoothly to the prince, currying favour with him, and then would present a very sad face to the king, weeping as if to show himself in accord with the royal opinion. Although Kim Sang-no wished to reveal his true mind to the king, he was unable to do so because Lady Sŏnhŭi was attending the king day and night in the royal bedroom, in addition to which attendant court ladies were constantly present. There were two bedrooms in the Kongmok-hap Pavilion mourner's hut, and the king lay next to the door of the inner room, while the three proctorial ministers and the royal doctor presented themselves in the outer room. So now Sang-no would prostrate himself just by the place where the king's head was resting, so that he could whisper secrets very quietly. But he was afraid of Lady Sŏnhŭi, who was serving the king in the inner room, and would scribble something on the floor with his hand. When he read what Kim Sang-no had written, the king would strike the threshold in exasperation and sigh, while Kim Sang-no was prostrate himself, weeping. Of course, any president of the council would cry bitterly under such circumstances, but Kim Sang-no was wickedly making mischief between the king and the prince — quite inhuman conduct. Lady Sŏnhŭi, who was always hobbling about in the background, saw him scribbling on the floor to convey his message to the king, and was mortified by his conduct, which she described as very wicked.

While the king was sick, our elder daughter was seriously ill with smallpox, but the disease eventually responded to treatment. The king himself recovered after the New Year, and came personally to see our daughter, which was an occasion for great celebration. In the third month, the king honoured my son with the title of royal grandson, and the royal grandson went to the Hyoso-jŏn Shrine and the Hwinyŏng-jŏn Shrine to pay homage. The crown prince, despite his sickness, was very pleased and proud of the title of royal grandson being bestowed upon his son. While he was scarcely aware of the existence of his wife and children during the more serious attacks of his illness, he was nevertheless immensely fond of the royal grandson and would never allow the princesses to dare to compete with him. He firmly and clearly defined the duties of those of lower birth, in order that they might show due respect to his son. When he acted like this, he did not seem at all ill.

The ceremonies connected with the three years' mourning period were completed on 31 May, and the ancestral tablet of Queen Dowager Inwŏn was placed in the Royal Ancestral Temple for the last time. I felt indescribably desolate. Prior to this, the board of rites had asked the king's permission to select a new queen. The king accordingly reported this to the Hyoso-jŏn shrine and decided to select a wife. The state wedding took place in the sixth month, at the time when the crown prince's condition was deteriorating rapidly. Although his illness was not publicly discussed, it was the cause of great concern. Lady Sŏnhŭi told me that, as Queen Chŏngsŏng had passed away, it was appropriate for the king to hold a state wedding and provide the kingdom with a new queen. She congratulated King Yŏngjo with utmost sincerity and prepared the state wedding in person. Her conduct in serving and protecting the royal person was completely beyond reproach. On the day following the wedding, when the crown prince and I had an audience with the king and queen at the queen's palace, the crown prince behaved with the utmost discretion lest he should give the impression of unfilial behaviour. This was just another instance of his innate sincerity and filial devotion.

In the intercalary sixth month of that year, the royal grandson celebrated his appointment as heir to the crown prince at the Myŏngjŏng-jŏn Audience Chamber. He was then eight years old: an outstanding, if rather solemn, little boy. On the face of things it would seem that, since the crown prince was deputizing for the king, while his son at the age of eight was celebrating his appointment as the royal grandson, the power of the state should have been as lofty and secure as Mount T'ai (*T'ae* in Korean), and nobody should have had any cause for anxiety. However, it was notoriously difficult to maintain a favourable position at court; nor was there any point in asking heaven for explanations of misfortunes.

During that autumn and winter the king was naturally engrossed in his new marriage and presented us with few difficulties. So we managed to get through that year fairly uneventfully, but in 1760 the crown prince's illness deteriorated yet more, and the king's rebukes daily increased in severity, with the result that the prince's temper was provoked more and more frequently, and his obsession with clothes became extreme. Suddenly he started to claim that he could see passers-by, who were in fact figments of his imagination, and he would send out servants to detain them while he was putting on his robes. But if the prince caught even the faintest glimpse of someone who did not move out of sight quickly enough, he could not keep wearing the same robe and felt compelled to change. If he wished to wear a silk military uniform, it was necessary to prepare a number of them, for he would often burn several before he felt he could continue wearing one. Thus, in 1759 and 1760, he burnt so many silk military uniforms that many chests of silk were wasted. Since they were all of the finest quality, I felt completely sick at heart.

It always seemed strange to me that the prince's birthday, on the twenty-first day of the first month, could never be celebrated in a peaceful, relaxed way. Instead, the king would hold a regular administrative board meeting on that day, or call for the royal instructor and ask about the crown prince's progress — actions which always saddened the prince. With the passing of the years he became increasingly depressed and anxious, so that on his birthday he was never able to enjoy the evening meal in a normal atmosphere. Eventually he came to insist on foregoing dinner on that day, so that the whole court would be upset. Alas, why was he dogged by such an awful fate!

On his birthday in 1760 he was so overwrought that he could not force himself to use the appropriate reverent language towards his parents; instead, he began to abuse them from that day on. He was in such a state that he seemed unable to distinguish between heaven and earth. As he felt there was no point in living any longer, he used a great deal of vulgar language to Lady Sŏnhŭi and screamed at the children when they came to make their greeting, saying, 'How do you expect me to be aware of my children, when I am not aware of my parents? Since I cannot fulfil my duty as a son, how can you expect me to do so as a father? Go away!' The children, who were then aged nine, seven and five years respectively, and were all dressed up in dragon-figured silk robes, crowns and belts in order to greet their father as he celebrated his birthday, were all frightened out of their wits by his fierce shouting. The scene was just too terrible to describe. Normally, although he was now really ill, he used to plague only me, and did not dare to offend his mother. Now Lady Sŏnhŭi, who had not really believed what I had told her about the prince's illness and thought I was exaggerating, saw for the first time what I meant, and was so terrified that she could not utter a word. The prince seemed completely unaware of his seventy-year-old mother, and even forgot his affection for his children. Lady Sŏnhŭi and the frightened children turned as pale as ashes. The whole incident was quite terrible, and I felt so upset that I was ready to kill myself. Yet I could not do so, and was so distraught that I appeared less than human.

Throughout the spring of that year, the prince's illness deteriorated steadily, and I never spent a moment free from anxiety. Then the king became concerned about the drought of the ensuing summer, saying that it was caused by the crown prince not cultivating virtue. He therefore rebuked the crown prince at great length with words too terrible to hear, which was too much for the sick prince to endure. Life seemed an endless succession of anxieties, and I felt I could not go on living even one moment under such circumstances. Day and night I simply wanted to die.

Though Madame Chŏng later behaved basely toward the royal grandson, she never refused to help the crown prince obtain a request, whatever it might be. If there was anything to blame in her conduct at this time, it was that she did not sacrifice herself to try to soften the king's feelings. From 1760 when the crown prince's condition began to deteriorate markedly, he began to tell Madame Chŏng to obtain various articles for him from the king, saying, 'Get me as much as you can!' Prior to this he had merely secretly asked her to obtain certain quantities of things for him. Now that his depression had deepened, he seemed to think that it was somehow the fault of Madame Chŏng that he was unable to enjoy the king's affection as she did, and his simmering resentment boiled over as he shouted, 'Make sure that everything works out well for me!' Madame Chŏng was completely terrified, but managed to keep the situation in hand.

According to what she told me, she was never quite sure of the king's reaction if she begged straightforwardly for whatever the prince had asked her to obtain, and so she would devise various schemes until she found one which would appease the prince without causing any trouble. The prince also asked her to prevent the king from calling him in to an audience, so that he might avoid the king's comments. And since he was worried lest something might happen while she was away from the court, he would shout out fearfully, 'I will not see you again if you stay away from the court.' So, for the time being, Madame Chŏng was not allowed to go home, and could not even be present to celebrate the coming-of-age of her adopted son, Hu-gyŏm, at the end of July 1760.

Every day saw a further worsening in the prince's condition, accompanied by his growing conviction of his inability to face the king. He felt he could not enjoy being in the same palace with the king, and wanted the king to move into another palace, for he felt that he would then be able to exorcise his resentful feelings by practising martial arts in the rear courtyard. Having made a sudden decision, he informed Madame Chŏng, 'I do not think I can live in the same palace with the king, so please take the king to the upper palace by any means you can, such as telling him that you want him to have a look at the upper palace or something like that.'

While the prince was making these plans, he had first asked me to tell Madame Chŏng what part he wanted her to play. He had threatened me in such a terrifying manner, that I felt my life was hanging by a thread! However, the princess managed to devise some way of persuading the king to move into the other palace, and he chose 18 August 1760 as an auspicious day for the move. On the 16th the prince summoned Madame Chŏng and said, with his hand on his sword, 'From now on, if anything happens to me, I will slash you with this sword.' Lady Sŏnhŭi, who had accompanied her daughter, fearing that she might come to some harm, was shocked and amazed by the sight.

The princess wept and begged him, 'Please spare my life, for I will do anything you ask from now on.'

The prince replied, 'I feel I am suffocating staying in this palace all the time. Will you persuade the king to allow me to go to Onyang? You know that my feet develop boils from the humidity during the summer.'

The princess answered, 'Yes, Sire,' and departed.

The king moved into the other palace and gave permission for the prince to proceed to Onyang. The princess must have made a fuss to see that things went smoothly — how otherwise could the king have moved into the other palace so suddenly, and have permitted the prince to proceed to Onyang, something quite unprecedented? Perhaps if she had striven as hard as this earlier to improve relations between father and son, things might have been better. But then, what could anyone do? It was heaven's will.

I was unable to go and make my farewells when the king departed, because the prince had thrown a chessboard at me, which had struck above the left eye so hard that I had almost lost my eye. Fortunately, no lasting damage was done, but I was left with a dreadful bruise and the eye itself was very swollen. I could not face Lady Sŏnhŭi for the same reason, and was startled to realize that there was no way of conveying my sad thoughts at her departure. All my efforts were now completely futile, and it seemed impossible to go on living. I wanted to die, but I could not do so, since I could not abandon the royal grandson. We moved from one crisis to another, and I am unable to record them all here.

When the king moved into the other palace, he ordered preparations to be made for the trip to Onyang, and the prince set out on 23 August. In motherly fashion, Lady Sŏnhŭi worried about his safe return, and missed him so much that she was always sending him food parcels which she had prepared. Her nephew, Yi In-gang, was a general in charge of Kongju, and she would ask him to send her news of how the prince was faring. He seemed to be constantly in her thoughts, which was only natural.

When the prince departed, the king was advised to allow him to go without saying farewell to him. The prince's progress to Onyang took place in a most desolate atmosphere. Although the prince would have wished to have been preceded by a number of guards, and to have been accompanied by a triumphant military band, he was unable to do so, since the king had only reluctantly permitted him to go. None of the prince's own men ever dared to say anything about relations between father and son.

Though I was extremely fond of my husband, I felt very relieved when he went away to Onyang. I enjoyed the respite from feeling that I was living constantly on the brink of disaster. I can hardly describe my father's concern over the situation, nor the awkwardness it caused in relations between my father and the prince. Father and I were consumed with anxiety day and night — a dismay which future generations may easily imagine. While the prince was away in Onyang, the royal grandson asked that his youngest uncle, Hong Nag-yun and his cousin Su-yŏng, should be summoned. Since it seemed that my own life might be cut off at any minute, my relatives, brothers and their wives came to say farewell.

The prince had looked as if his last hour was about to come while he was making the final preparations for his departure for Onyang, but by the time he had passed through the city gate his fury had abated so much that he ordered that none of his train should disturb the people along the way, while he himself acted with great dignity and bestowed favours on the people. He was cheered by those he passed, who called him 'brilliant prince'. After he settled in the royal lodge at Onyang, all the people there came under the influence of his virtue. The whole town became very peaceful and secure, and the people admired the prince's virtue and invoked his name. I hoped his illness might have disappeared in this flush of enthusiasm, and that his sickness would give place to his innate good nature. But though he travelled all the way to Onyang, he found the town very small and without any scenic attraction, or much less magnificent scenic attraction!

After staying there for about ten days he again felt depressed, and returned to his palace on 14 September 1760. Then he declared that he would like to go to P'yŏngsan, because Onyang had been stifling. However, it was impossible to ask the king's permission for a further move, so I persuaded him not to go, telling him that P'Yŏngsan was narrower and more cramped than Onyang. He was in a complete quandary, with the royal instructors and subordinates continually urging him, 'Please have an audience with the king.' But he was not fit to see the king, and this caused me much concern.

The king kept the royal grandson near him a great deal. The king was concerned about everything and would talk only of his anxieties at council meetings. It was natural for him to praise the royal grandson, and his confidence in him was such that he intended to entrust him with the kingdom. He often expressed his affection for his grandson, for he was clever and precocious and his behaviour and response suited the king's disposition. The crown prince used to ask the court annalist to record for him the speeches made at council meetings, and to read them to him. But when he came upon such phrases as 'the king praised and made much of the royal grandson, saying "I will entrust the royal grandson with the most important responsibility of the state",' he was extremely disturbed.

79

The crown prince loved the royal grandson, but since relations between father and son had never been easy in the royal family, he became sick with resentment when he realized, despite his illness, that the king praised only the royal grandson, while he himself had from childhood not once received a mark of the king's affection. Since the future of the country depended on the royal grandson, and it was necessary for the safety of the kingdom to ensure his well-being, I worked out a way to keep him secure. This was to prevent the crown prince from reading the reports. However, since it was impossible to prevent the prince from reading any of them, I sent a message to the eunuchs telling them to alter, before the prince could read them, any parts of the royal speeches where the king praised the royal grandson. Sometimes, when it was urgent, I myself asked the eunuchs to cut out such passages. I told my father about this and asked him, 'Please find some way to ensure the royal grandson's safety.'

My father, acting out of the deepest loyalty towards the state, carefully arranged that such passages should not be included when reports of the council meetings were written. Confronted with this most difficult situation, father tried to repay the royal favour he had received by protecting the royal grandson without jeopardizing the prince. At times the strain became too much for him, and his nerves were so upset that he became continually sick. Whenever he saw me he prayed to heaven for the peace of the country, and above all that the royal grandson might be saved so that he could inherit the kingdom — and for this it was essential that the crown prince should not read such passages. Father and I were naturally very worried about this point, and our agonized efforts were plain to everyone. If the crown prince had seen the king's words of praise for the royal grandson in the original, you could never imagine what dreadful things might have happened.

The prince's illness continued to worsen throughout 1761. Since the king had moved into the other palace the prince had spent his days riding and exercising with weapons in the rear courtyard. But after August 1760 he became tired of doing this all the time and suddenly started to go into town in disguise. I cannot find words to describe my initial shock.

The prince could not help killing people when he was suffering from an attack of his illness. Hyŏn-ju's mother, Ping-ae, used to take care of the prince's robes, and one day in the first month, 1761, just as the prince was about to change his robes in order to travel incognito, he suffered a sudden attack of his illness and beat Ping-ae so severely that he injured her critically. He went out and Ping-ae died at the palace not long after. It was a tragedy not only for Ping-ae herself, but also for her children, who were so wretchedly bereaved!

Since the king might visit at any time, we could not keep the body in the palace for even a little while, and indeed we felt pressed to keep it overnight. We sent it out in the morning and arranged for the funeral to be held at the Yongdon-gung Palace, providing plenty of money for the funeral expenses. When the prince came home and heard about this he said nothing. He seemed to be in a state of stupor, and everything he did is just too awful to describe. He spent the whole period between the second and third month roaming about incognito, making frequent trips in and out of the palace. I was quite terrified and fearful of the outcome. In the third month the royal grandson entered the institute of the royal grandson and celebrated his coming-of-age at Kyŏnghŭi Palace. Although I longed to attend the celebration, the crown prince was not fit to go, and I was not brave enough to go on my own. So I stayed away, saying I was sick.

Between 24 February and 23 April the president of the council, Yi Ch'ŏn-bo, and two vice presidents of the council, Yi Hu and Min Paek-sang, killed themselves in quick succession.[3] Then the king fell ill, and as there were no senior ministers my father was appointed the president of the council. In view of his personal situation and that of the state as a whole, he was not at all willing to take up office. However, realizing that the state had no one to direct it, he assumed office in the third month, thus conforming to his principle of accepting the pleasures and the hardships of his station. So fixed was his determination to serve his country, that he was prepared to do his best even if it meant his death. This was an extremely anxious time for him.

On about 4 May 1761, the prince travelled incognito to P'yŏngyang. The then governor of P'yŏngan province was Chŏng Hwi-ryang, an uncle by marriage of Princess Hwawan, and the prince was confident that his deeds would not be reported to the king. The governor knew that the prince would not inform him of his arrival, but felt that he could not just remain in his office as if nothing had happened. He therefore presented himself and offered to supply food and whatever else the prince required for his stay. It is said that the governor was so concerned that he vomited blood.

He was a very cautious man, and since Prince Ilsŏng was already dead, he was very worried in view of the fact that the king loved Princess Hwawan more than any of his other children. It must have been a very trying time for him.

After the prince left for P'yŏngyang I was overwhelmed with worry, while father was so overwrought that he secretly sought news of the prince from the governor. He remained almost constantly at the palace, merely going home to sit in his front hall throughout the night. He must have been in a terrible state! It was quite out of the question for him to report the prince's doings to the king, and he was therefore unable to remonstrate. If circumstances had allowed him to expostulate with the king, he certainly would have done so. But even had he done so, the king would not have listened, and father's offence might have jeopardized my life and even the security of the children. So it was not that he did not want to remonstrate about the matter, but rather that, in view of the crown prince's hopeless condition, he was concerned most of all to protect the royal grandson. People who did not understand the situation rather blamed my father for not leading the king in the right direction, but there was no one to whom he could explain the situation. It was distressing that he had to face such opposition.

About twenty days after the prince left for P'yŏngyang, sometime around 24 May 1761, he returned to the palace. It was almost a relief, after the agonies of worry that I had endured. While the prince was away it was decided to pretend that he was sick and one of the eunuchs was persuaded to impersonate him. So this eunuch, Yu In-sik, lay in bed in the prince's inner chamber, imitating his voice, while another eunuch, Pak Mun-hung, did as he was told in everything. I was terrified by all this, and what happened is too awful to be recorded here. At length a letter of complaint was sent to the court by Yun Chae-gyŏm. Though it would have been proper for father to remonstrate with the king about the letter, the prince was not in a fit condition to discuss the matter. If the king was told, anything could have happened. So father was unable to remonstrate.

Since returning from his trip to P'yŏngyang the prince seemed in better control of himself and attended the regular administrative board meeting and even resumed his studies. I hoped that he might settle down after all; but it was pitiful to have such hopes. Later, at the regular administrative board meeting, Kyehŭi mentioned something about the prince's misconduct, which drew a firm rebuke from the prince, who cited the example of Chiang Ch'ung.[4] This led

82

father to hope that the prince might have recovered from his illness, and he came joyfully to tell me what had happened at the meeting. After 12 June 1761 the prince went to the Kyŏnghŭi Palace and, for the first time, paid homage without any trouble, thank heaven. About the middle of that month I also went to the Kyŏnghŭi Palace with the royal grandson to see the king and Lady Sŏnhŭi. Lady Sŏnhŭi was so upset that she could find nothing to say to me.

From spring of that year the prince suffered an attack of malaria, which lasted for several months and which kept him constantly upset and disturbed. I felt that it was due to the abuse he had inflicted on his person, as the disease dated from the time of his incognito travels. If only he had died from the disease then, I would have had to experience only the agony of losing him; but he was to survive it and experience a succession of disasters unparalleled since ancient times. It may sound inhuman to talk in this way, but if he had died at this time, the distress of the children and myself, the terrible upheavals, and the attendant suffering and resentment of my own family, would never have reached the proportions they did. I cannot understand the workings of heaven.

The prince recovered from malaria in the eighth month, 1761, and around the ninth month of the same year the king made a visit to our palace. He had at last found out about the crown prince's trip to P'yŏngyang, due to a memorial presented by Sŏ Myŏng-ŭng. This had been recorded in the diary of the royal secretariat, where it had been read by the king, who thus discovered what had been going on. However, although we experienced some upheavals, thanks to the help of Chŏng Hwi-ryang we avoided a major calamity. Since the king was about to proceed to the Ch'angdŏk Palace to regularize the administration of the eunuchs, he had time to do nothing more than reproach the prince. Experience from childhood had shown me that, although the king would examine insignificant matters very closely and fastidiously, if the trouble was too serious to be dealt with by merely making a fuss, he would be less furious than he was over minor problems — just as on the occasion when he was told that the prince had been killing people and he had comforted his son, and explained that he had acted like this because he had been hurt. So, after finding out about the prince's trip to P'yŏngyang, instead of flying into a rage and punishing him severely, he deplored it less than might have been expected. I felt that he was not sure how to handle the problem.

Then a royal procession was announced and the prince put away all his weapons which had been scattered about the palace. He was then staying in the Hwanch'wi-jŏn Mansion and, believing that he would not be safe from the king, he spoke to me with an affection he had not displayed for many years, asking my advice about what he should do, as he felt himself to be in danger. Quite overcome, I answered, 'However annoyed he is, the king will hardly take any drastic action.'

The prince retorted, 'Not so! The king loves the royal grandson and since he has him, it would make no difference to him if he finished me off.'

I answered, 'Since the royal grandson is your son, surely the happiness and misfortune of both of you is bound together, isn't it?'

He replied, 'You are not thinking straight. The king hates me so much that things are getting very difficult. He will destroy me and make the royal grandson the adopted son of Crown Prince Hyojang, and there is nothing we can do about it.'

He did not look ill as he said this, but spoke so sadly that I felt very depressed and murmured, 'It is hardly possible.'

He then said, 'Wait and see! Though you belong to me, the king has treated you and the children quite normally, but he has hated me, and me alone, so much that I have fallen into this state, and it is hardly possible that he will let me live now.'

I was so distressed to hear these words that I wept, and when I was undergoing the pain and agony of the event of 1764, I remembered what the prince had said and thought it was very strange that he had in those words so clearly foreseen the future. The knowledge that he was gifted with such a penetrating insight served to intensify the resentment I felt.

The king, however, was unable to make the procession at that time and so the prince felt more at ease, although every such crisis served to worsen his condition, and so in the tenth month 1761, he was worse again, which was a great sorrow.

It was at this time that the selection of a wife for the royal grandson was fixed. Father once told me that he had seen the future queen as a child, when he had been invited to the sixtieth anniversary of the mother of the board minister, Kim Sŏng-ŭng, and that even then he had regarded her as having an exceptional character. The crown prince saw the name of the daughter of the deputy board minister, Kim Si-mok, on the list of daughters of eligible government officials, and was very much inclined to select her. He sent a message to the princess to say, 'See to it that the king selects her, otherwise you will get into trouble.' However, the opinion of the king, as well as that of the court, inclined towards the daughter of Yun Tŭg-yang. As the crown prince was not able to attend the selection, I too was unable to go, which was a most distressing experience for a mother whose affection for her son far exceeded that of an ordinary mother. The crown prince was very anxious about the outcome, and was quite delighted when he was told that the decision had been made in favour of the daughter of Kim Si-mok.

Soon after the second selection, the royal grandson's wife-to-be contracted measles, as did the royal grandson not long afterwards. However, he recovered about 4 January 1762. The king was delighted, since he had been anxious about the illness, and the prince too was so relieved and behaved with such discretion that it seemed he was not ill any longer. I prayed secretly with clasped hands to the gods of heaven and earth, that because of my own special affection they might save him from the serious disease. Father too displayed his noble nature, doing night duty in the palace, and words cannot describe the extent of his exertions. Both the royal grandson and his wife-elect recovered without much trouble, thanks to the help of the royal ancestors.

The third selection was set for January 1762. I was looking forward tremendously to this event, for they could but show the girl to the parents of the royal grandson, and the king accordingly called for the crown prince and myself. I was very glad to be able to see the royal grandson's wife-elect, but on the other hand I was very worried as to how the prince would react to the occasion. Of course, it turned out just as I feared. The prince, in his usual fashion, put on several sets of robes, one after the other, destroying each set which he decided he could not wear, and did the same thing with his hats. Consequently, he went to the ceremony wearing two jade beads appropriate to an official of the third rank on his hat strings, instead of the jade strings befitting a senior official, which we could no longer afford. The king and prince met at Sahyŏn-hap Pavilion. I was aware that the meeting between them would not pass without trouble, but the king had summoned him in order that he would be present at a major event in the life of his own son. When there were much more serious matters at stake, why should it have mattered if the prince's jade ornaments were too big and ugly, like those of a military officer, even though it made him look hardly a crown prince? The king was so upset about the beads that he ordered the prince to go back without seeing the girl, and even before she came in, at which I was very downcast. I felt that the king should have acted differently. The prince must have felt terrible returning without even being able to see his future daughter-in-law, and I wondered how he managed to do so obediently, without a show of anger. I myself decided to see the royal grandson's wife before I went back, even though it could have cost me my life. So I managed to see the third selection, but I thought it very cruel that the prince should not be able to do so.

I was very worried about the incident that happened to the prince, so I said to the queen, Lady Sŏnhŭi and the princess, 'As the way to the Detached Palace is through the Ch'angdŏk Palace, I was wondering about taking her and introducing her to the prince without telling the king.' They all agreed that it was a good idea, and so I told the eunuchs in attendance, 'When you pass the lower palace, bring the girl's palanquin in together with mine.' So I took her to the prince, who was in a most unhappy mood, having been sent home without even being able to see his daughter-in-law. He was lying resting in the Tŏksŏng-hap Pavilion, sad and dumb-founded. I said, 'I have brought the royal grandson's wife-to-be, Sire.' He rejoiced to see her, caressed her happily, and did not send her to the Detached Palace until nightfall. I had brought her to see the prince because the situation was so desperate, but I regretted having to deceive the king.

The prince was becoming more and more depressed and his condition was deteriorating every day. It was quite incredible, and most embarrassing, to hear the disrespectful way in which he referred to the king. My every moment was haunted with fear, and I wanted the state wedding to hurry on, for I was uncertain how much longer I had to live. The New Year came round and the state wedding was fixed for 25 February 1762. While I was worrying about how we would get through the wedding without any trouble, the prince's tonsils suddenly became infected, some time after 3 February. This was a very serious condition, and I was very worried, since the state wedding was so close. However, he recovered immediately after having acupuncture, which was most fortunate.

The wedding date drew closer, and the king sent first for the royal grandson. So he went first, and the prince left soon after for the Kyŏnghyŏn-dang Hall, resting outside the Sŭnghyŏn Gate. Thus it came about that the royal grandson went through the wedding ceremony at the Kyŏnghyŏn-dang Hall, where three generations, father, son and grandson, were gathered together in one hall.

Having celebrated his grandson's wedding, the king sent him to the bride's home for the wedding rites — a very happy and solemn occasion, as well as an immensely joyful one. After the wedding ceremony, the wedding reception was held at Kwangmyŏng-jŏn Mansion and the prince stayed in Chŭphŭi-dang Hall, while both the royal grandson and his wife spent the night at Kwangmyŏng-jŏn Mansion.

The next day the king, the queen, the prince and myself had an audience with the royal grandson and his wife. The king and queen were seated on the north wall of the Kwangmyŏng-jŏn Mansion, while the prince was placed on the east side and myself on the west. The royal grandson's bride was having some difficulty with her heavy coiffure and formal wedding costume which she was too young to manage, and so the king and the prince had to sit facing each other for quite a long time while she made her slow entrance. The king felt ill at ease facing the prince, but tolerated the situation, although he looked most unhappy about it, especially since he could not find any excuse to blame the prince. I was mentally praying that the king would not say anything, and went out to hurry my new daughter-in-law in. I also hastened the preparation of the meal, which was served to both the king and the queen — fortunately, without incident.

The crown prince felt awkward throughout his stay there, but did not want to leave before the three days that the royal grandson and his bride were in residence. Indeed, his illness was not apparent at this time, and if he had been better treated, he might still have improved himself. However, the king, who had been obliged to allow the prince to attend such an important ceremony as the royal wedding reception, now ordered him to leave, but insisted on my staying on for a further three days after the audience had been completed. Nevertheless, since there were numerous reasons why it would be very awkward for me to stay on, I managed to make some excuse and left soon afterwards, following the prince. The royal grandson and his wife came to Ch'angdŏk Palace after three days, and the prince, who had been waiting for them, rejoiced to see them and took his royal daughter-in-law to Hwinyŏng-jŏn Shrine to pay homage to the Ancestral Temple. He himself was moved a great deal. When he undertook such actions, he seemed to be once more in possession of his true self, and he favoured this daughter-in-law so exceptionally that although she was still very young when the prince died, she was very upset and came to cherish his memory more and more as time went by, weeping each time his name was mentioned, not only because she had been so favoured, but also she had a very loyal nature.

These days, the prince never met his father-in-law privately, but when father left for North Hamgyŏng province, at the request of the king, to pay homage to one of the royal tombs, the king told me to ask father to see the new bride before he left. When father went to the lower palace he was met by the prince, who was feeling better that day and who, moreover, wished to boast of his new daughter-in-law. From his earliest years the prince had never had any relatives whom he could meet privately, and had to be content with the royal assistant or the royal instructors. Therefore, he was never intimate with anyone outside the court until our marriage, when he met father, with whom he became very friendly. Though father used to come to see the king at the beginning and the middle of every month, he came to see us only when instructed to do so by the king, and even when he did come he would not stay long, saying, 'Since the palace is governed by strict regulations, a commoner should not stay too long.'

But whenever he had an audience with the prince, he would urge him to study hard and would help him with his history lessons, frequently citing passages from the writings of men of former times. He would review and make critical comments on any compositions which the prince sent to him, so that the prince learnt a lot from father. No other subject could have prayed even a fraction as earnestly as he did for the prince to be a good and wise king with a long and peaceful reign. He loved the prince immensely, and always helped guide him towards the right. Other relatives occasionally gave the prince toys to play with, but father never did so, confining himself to repeating, 'Please improve your filial piety!' or 'Please study hard!' He would hardly say anything apart from these two phrases, and the prince held him in great awe and respect. Even now, though his health was deteriorating, he did not say anything to father's face and at times when I found the situation quite unbearable, I would write to father begging, 'Please help the prince, as he is going through one of his difficult phases. I am relying on you to do so.'

The prince himself, however, never wrote, and even when his life hung in the balance because of his clothes fixation, it was I who asked my father to obtain the material, for the prince would never

88

have begged it from him. Although he took from Prince Kùmsòng and Madame Chòng, he never begged from my family. When he started to travel incognito, it might have seemed natural for him to go to my home first, but he would go to Prince Kùmsong's and prepare himself there — never to my home. He either showed great deference towards father or avoided him, but never treated him rudely. Indeed, he felt embarrassed about his secret trips and the change which had come over him, and could not face my father and talk to him. He used to meet father at the regular administrative board meeting, or when deputizing for the king when the latter was ill, but he did not see father in private for many years. So now father was delighted to have an audience with the prince, and congratulated him on obtaining a daughter-in-law while still so young himself, and on being able to enjoy the happiness of hosting his son and his wife. The prince was very pleased by this, and played the perfect host to my father just as he used to. There was not a slightest trace of his illness, which was very strange.

In the third month, 1762, he was again subjected to a great deal of criticism, which caused his condition to deteriorate again so rapidly until it became quite hopeless. I find myself at a loss to describe the situation. During his fits of rage, he would force the court maids and eunuchs to call out things which they would otherwise never had dared to have spoken. But in fear of their lives, they loudly shouted out the immoral words. Life was so difficult for me that I wanted to die and escape from everything. Before this, the prince had never drunk wine, and I had been very resentful about the wine incident of 1756. As the king had told him on that occasion, wine had always been strictly prohibited in the court. The prince, however, began to have quantities of wine brought in. Though he could not drink very much, for his own drinking capacity was quite poor, a great deal of wine had been stored inside the royal palace and its presence there was a constant source of great anxiety.

After 1760, the prince killed a great number of court maids and eunuchs and I cannot remember all their names. One whose name sticks in my memory is Sò Kyòng-dal, the palace treasurer. The prince killed him because he did not carry out the prince's orders quickly enough. He also killed many of the eunuchs on duty, and even one of the court maids from Lady Sònhùi's palace, so that life became unbearable.

On his secret trip to P'yŏngyang in 1761, the prince had brought back with him a nun and a *kisaeng*,[5] whom he kept at the court. He would hold parties with them, and other servant girls and *kisaengs* would come in from outside to take part in the orgies — a sight which had never been seen before in all the past history of the country. At the end of March 1762, the prince invited the Princess Hwawan, Madame Chŏng, to come and made free with her whenever he wanted to, saying that it was because his illness made him so depressed. The princess, frightened and embittered, swore at him. I was terrified to death, and dared not listen or pay any attention. On one occasion the prince entertained the princess at T'ongmyŏng-jŏn Mansion. Places he selected for such parties were always either the courtyard at the rear of the palace or the T'ongmyŏng-jŏn Mansion, and he sometimes stayed overnight in the Hwanch'wi-jŏn Mansion.

So an anxious third month gave way to a fourth month. Nothing in the prince's quarters seemed appropriate to a living person. It resembled the apartment where a dead body is kept before burial. He set up a red flag, similar to the flag inscribed with the name and rank of people, and slept in a place which looked like a bier. After one of his late night parties, everyone would fall asleep exhausted, leaving the table full of food, so that the messy sight was reminiscent of the aftermath of a feast by ghosts. However, since this was heaven's will, there was nothing one could do.

The prince sometimes put to death even the blind fortune-tellers who were asked to tell his fortune, if they foretold something unlucky. He also killed or maimed royal physicians, translators and court workmen, so that every day several dead bodies were carried out of the palace. Everyone, both inside and outside the court, was in a fearful state of anxiety, and everyone was on tenterhooks, not knowing when they might be killed. The prince had now lost his good nature and lofty natural disposition, and had turned completely bad — more so, in fact, than I can describe.

Suddenly, in the fifth month, he started excavating and in the cavity built a house with three rooms, putting in sliding doors between each room, so that it looked just like the inside of a grave. The door was situated on the ceiling, giving just enough space for the people to creep in between the top panel and the door, and the top panel was then covered with grass so that there was no sign of the house built underneath. The prince was very pleased with his work, and shut himself up in the house, which was lighted by a hanging jade lamp. All this was done simply to provide somewhere to hide weapons and even horses, in case the king came to visit and investigate what the prince was doing. Rumours about it ran wild. The prince seemed as if possessed by a spirit, which human power would never be able to control.

That month, for the first time since the royal grandson's wedding, Lady Sŏnhŭi came to the lower palace, partly to see us, and partly to see her grand-daughter-in-law. The prince was very pleasant and affectionate towards her, and indeed treated her extravagantly. He probably guessed that this would be his last meeting with her, so the daily meal and the banquet table were sumptuous, with the fruit piled high and even ginseng cake. The prince composed a poem on the theme of long life and poured wine for his mother. Attention was lavished on her, and when she was taken to the courtyard at the rear of the palace, the prince prepared a palanquin like that of the king and forced Lady Sŏnhŭi to mount inside. A flag was attached to the front of the palanquin, while retainers blew trumpets and beat drums — the prince's idea of the utmost filial piety. Lady Sŏnhŭi, however, was extremely shocked, realizing that there was less hope every day, and that things would eventually reach a completely unbelievable conclusion. Whenever she saw me she burst into tears saying, 'What will happen to him?' She barely managed to force herself to stay for a few days with us, and then went back to the upper palace, weeping. The prince also felt very sad: probably he was aware that it was the final farewell. I, too, felt grief-stricken at the possibility that I might not see Lady Sŏnhŭi alive again, in face of the growing danger and disturbance in the state.

The president of the council at this time was Sin Man, who had just finished a period of mourning and taken up his presidential post. The king, who had been unable to see him for three years, was as happy as if he was seeing him for the first time, and talked only about the prince, displaying great bitterness from beginning to end. The prince, who knew that his faults were being discussed, avoided Sin Man and then came to fear him, saying, 'The president of the council is unlucky; I hate him.' He gnashed his teeth, suspecting that Sin Man might have laid a false charge against him to the king, and wrought himself into a quite indescribable fury. I was at my wits' end and did not know what to do. Then quite unexpectedly the Na Kyŏng-ŏn Incident occurred.[6]

My cousin on my mother's side, Yi Hae-jung, was then a

secretary of the board of punishment. That wretched Sang-ŏn, a court guard and brother of Kyŏng-ŏn, did an awful thing out of malice, and made matters worse. The king questioned Kyŏng-ŏn and summoned the prince. He hastened to the upper palace on foot, presenting an indescribable spectacle. That wicked man Sang-ŏn thus served to aggravate the prince's illness and further harmed relations between father and son. Kyŏng-ŏn was condemned to death, while the prince had Sang-ŏn seized and brought in to be tortured in the Sŏnji-gak Audience Chamber courtyard in the Simin-dang Hall. He tried to make him reveal the name of the man who had persuaded him to report the affair to the king — which, however, he refused to do. So the prince's hatred towards Sin Man intensified and he said, 'I will seize the royal son-in-law, Prince Yŏng-sŏng, and kill him for what his father did.' The situation was extremely tense, with the servants telling the prince that they would bring in Prince Yŏngsŏng that day, and then the next. But Prince Yŏngsŏng, who probably was not fated to die then, was not brought in soon enough.

Lady Sŏnhŭi, who had viewed with despair the prince's growing wild behaviour, now reached the conclusion that she could not help him any more. Moreover, a letter he sent to Princess Hwawan, who was not acceding to his request, was so horrible that no one would have dared to repeat the words in it. He even said that he would get to her at the upper palace by going through a gutter. He was increasingly determined to kill Prince Yŏngsŏng. However, no one succeeded in bringing Prince Yŏngsŏng to the court, and only his official robe, his ceremonial robes for his audience with the king, his military uniform, his utensils for daily use and the ceremonial strings decorated with jade for his ceremonial robe, together with a gold crown and belt, were brought in. The prince had all these burnt and destroyed. Prince Yŏngsŏng's death now seemed imminent. Since Lady Sŏnhŭi felt there could be no further doubt that the prince's actions had reached a quite intolerable extreme, and not because she merely wished to save Prince Yŏngsŏng's life, she decided to advise the king to put the prince to death.

Between 2 and 3 July 1762, the prince tried in vain to get to the upper palace through a gutter. Frightful rumours abounded, which completely exaggerated the facts. The prince was so disturbed that all his actions were the product of madness. Thus, when he lost his senses and was possessed by anger, he insisted that he had to do it and said, 'I would go and do so with sword in hand.' I do not think he would have behaved like this even for one minute had he been in his right mind. His fate was so strange and cruel, that he had to experience things hitherto unknown, even from ancient times, and was not destined to live out his allotted span. Did heaven create such a disaster in order to make him suffer like that? Oh heaven, how can you inflict such things on the world?

Lady Sŏnhŭi felt unable to blame her sick son, but recognized that she could no longer rely on him. Since he was her only son and her only support in the world, she would never have made such a recommendation as this to the king, if the situation had not reached such a critical stage. It was Lady Sŏnhŭi's lifelong torment that her son's condition had developed because he was unable to receive the king's favour, and that the king was never able to overcome his prejudice. Even when the prince's affliction became so severe that he could not recognise his parents, she still hesitated to offer any advice to the king because of her own feelings towards the prince. Yet all the time she was alarmed that he might become involved in some unimaginable disaster, being in such a state that he was totally unaware of what he was doing. And what would happen then to the four-hundred-year-old dynasty? She therefore decided that it was right to protect the king, even though this meant that the prince should not continue to live, in view of the fact that his illness was so critical and that the royal grandson was a blood relative of the three royal ancestors. It was for these reasons that she concluded there was no other way to protect the kingdom, even though her love for the prince knew no bound.

On 4 July 1762 she wrote to me, saying, 'Since the rumours about what happened last night were so much more serious than anything I have heard before, I felt I would rather have been dead than have heard them. If I must live, it is only right for me to protect the kingdom and save the royal grandson, although I do not think I shall be able to face you again for the rest of my life.' This was the full extent of her note, and I wept as I held her letter in my hand, not knowing the great tragedy that would occur that day.

On the morning of that same day, the king was in the Kwan'gwang-ch'ŏng Hall at Kyŏnghyŏn-dang Mansion, and was just about to seat himself on the throne to hold audience. Lady Sŏnhŭi approached him and said weeping, 'Since the prince's illness has become quite critical and his case is hopeless, it is only proper that you should protect yourself and the royal grandson, in order to keep the kingdom at peace. I request that you eliminate the prince, even though such a suggestion is outrageous and a sin against humanity.' She added, 'It would be terrible for a father to do this in view of the bond of affection between father and son; but it is his illness which is to be blamed for this disaster, and not the prince himself. Though you eliminate him, please exert your benevolence to save the royal grandson, and allow him and his mother to live in peace.'

It was impossible for me, as the prince's wife, to admit that she was right, but the situation was completely hopeless. It would have been proper for me to have followed the prince in death, but I could not bring myself to do so because of the royal grandson, and I lamented the cruel necessity of continuing to live.

When the king received Lady Sŏnhŭi's recommendation, he did not give himself time to think over the decision, but hurriedly ordered a procession to Ch'angdŏk Palace. Lady Sŏnhŭi herself, having made a supreme sacrifice of her love for the benefit of the state, was totally distraught, beating her breast with her hands. She went to Yangdŏk-dang Hall where she used to live, and lay there without food, presenting an example of suffering rarely seen since ancient times.

Traditionally, there were two ways for the king to proceed to the Sŏnwŏn-jŏn Hall: if he took the way through the Manan Gate, it meant that there would be no trouble; but when he took the way through the Kyŏnghwa Gate, it always indicated that something unpleasant would happen. On that day he ordered his procession to pass through the Kyŏnghwa Gate. The prince had got himself soaking wet on the night of 2 July, going to and from the upper palace through the gutter, and on 3 July he had stayed in the T'ongmyong-jŏn Mansion. One of the beams of that building made a great noise, as if it were about to break. The prince, on hearing this, sighed and said, 'What is the matter? Perhaps I am going to be killed.' Father had been dismissed in June 1762 from his position as president of the council, and had been given firm instructions that he should remain in the eastern suburbs for about a month. The prince, who must have sensed danger, asked his bodyguard, Cho Yu-jin, to send a message to fetch former junior vice president of the council, Cho Chae-ho, who was then in Ch'unch'ŏn. He did not look at all sick as he did this. How strange are the workings of heaven!

The prince was terrified to hear of the king's arrival, and ordered that his weapons and horses should be put out of sight as planned. He then returned to the Kyŏngch'un-jŏn Mansion in a palanquin, telling me to follow him there. Whenever he went anywhere, he used to have a cover put on the palanquin and curtains hung round on all sides, to deter him from his habit of attacking anyone he saw. He pretended to the royal instructor and others that he was suffering from malaria.

It was about noon when the prince asked me to come to Tŏksŏng-hap Audience Chamber, and then suddenly a great cawing flock of magpies surrounded the Kyŏngch'un-jŏn Mansion. What sort of omen was this! I felt a strange premonition, and thought of the royal grandson who was away in the Hwan'gyŏng-jŏn Mansion. I felt very concerned about what might have happened to him, and so went to him and said, 'Whatever may happen please do not be frightened. Instead, show how strong you can be!' Not knowing what else to do, I kept repeating my request for him to take care of himself.

The king's procession was somehow delayed, and it was announced that he would come to Hwinyŏng-jŏn Shrine at three o'clock in the afternoon. The prince, in the meantime, had urged me to go to the Tŏksŏng-hap Audience Chamber. When I went there I found him sitting, leaning against the wall and meditating, with his head bowed. He looked frightened and pale. I had imagined that he would have flown into a rage at the sight of me, and certainly have ill-treated me. This was why I had warned the royal grandson to look after himself, thinking that I might be killed by the prince that day. But in fact the prince acted in a way quite the opposite to my anticipations, saying, 'I have a strange feeling that they will let you live. Their intentions are all so horrible!'

I received this remark in silence, with tears in my eyes, my hands nervously catching at each other, and my mind full of all sorts of preposterous thoughts. Then it was announced that the king had arrived at the Hwinyŏng-jŏn Shrine, and wished the prince to present himself. To my amazement the prince did not say, 'Let us go and hide!' or 'Let us run away!' Without any show of anger or performance of any kind, he asked me to bring the royal robe straight away. When he was attired in it, he said, 'Bring me the royal grandson's winter cap, because I am going to say that I have caught malaria.' I asked one of the court maids to bring his own winter cap, for I thought the royal grandson's cap would be too small for the prince. At this, the prince suddenly and unexpectedly exclaimed, 'You really are a horrible person! Just because you want to go on living for a long time beside the royal grandson, you hesitate to give his winter cap to someone who is going to be killed.

Of course I can imagine your resentment.'

I could not believe that he would be killed, and felt anxious lest my own life and that of my son might have been jeopardized for some imaginary reason. But hearing such totally unexpected words from the prince, I felt most depressed, and so brought him the royal grandson's winter cap, saying, 'You have completely misconstrued my thoughts, so please wear this one.'

He retorted, 'No, I won't. Why should I wear something which you resented giving to me?' This did not sound at all like the words of a sick man. Why, alas! did he go so obediently? It must have been heaven's will!

Meanwhile it was getting dark and he hurried to the king, who was seated in the Hwinyŏng-jŏn Shrine, grasping a sword in his hand. There the king finally took the decision to kill the prince, striking the floor (in his anger). It is impossible for me to describe the sight. Alas, it was most tragic! As soon as the prince had left me I could hear the angry voice of the king, so I sent someone to keep watch under the wall of the Hwinyŏng-jŏn Shrine, which is not far from where I was at the Tŏksŏng-hap Pavilion, and this person reported to me that the prince was already prostrating himself, with his royal robe taken off. I realized immediately that it was a situation of the utmost gravity and felt my heart torn asunder. Since it was pointless to stay there, I went to the royal grandson. Neither of us knew what to do, and we remained together, embracing each other. At about four o'clock it was reported that a eunuch had come to ask for the large grain box from the kitchen outside the Taejo-jŏn Mansion. This request was hard to understand, and put us in such a fluster that we could not readily obey the order. The royal grandson, guessing that matters had reached a climax, went inside the gate to the king and said, 'Please save my father!'

The king very sternly said, 'Go away!' Whereupon the royal grandson came and sat down in the prince's anteroom. I doubt that anyone, from the beginning of the world, has experienced such feelings as I did then. After I had seen the royal grandson out, I felt as if heaven and earth had collided and the sun and the moon had gone into eclipse, and I had no further wish to remain in this world. I tried to kill myself with a sword, but I could not succeed: there were people around me who snatched it away. A second attempt was also fruitless, since I could not find anything sharp enough. I went and stood under the Kŏnbok Gate, which leads to the Hwinyŏng-jŏn Shrine through the Sŭngmun-dang Hall, but could not see anything. I could only hear the king banging his sword against the floor, and the prince saying, 'Father, father, please do not do this! I know I did wrong, but from now on I will do my reading and whatever you wish me to do. I will do just as you wish!' Once again I felt my heart torn apart, and my vision blurred. It was no use struggling, or beating my breast with my hands.

With his physical courage and manly strength, why did the prince not resist going into the grain box, when he was forced to do so? Instead, he simply submitted to be put in. At first he tried to run away, but he could not fight his way out in such circumstances. How could heaven bring him to this?

Though I was wailing under the gate, in the grip of a bitter and unprecedented sorrow, there was no response. Since the crown prince was already dethroned, it would be difficult for his wife and children to stay at court. Also, I was worried about keeping the royal grandson out there, in case something might happen. Therefore, sitting at the gate, I wrote a memorial to the king saying, 'In view of your feelings, it is impossible for us to remain at court, and it would be most inappropriate to keep the royal grandson here, since he shares his father's guilt. Therefore, we beg permission to go to my family's house, and I entreat Your Highness to extend your favour to the royal grandson and to protect him.' I had great trouble finding a eunuch to hand the note to the king.

Before long my brother came and said, 'You are not to stay at the court, since you have been demoted to commoner status, and you have been instructed to return home. We have brought the palanquin for you and another palanquin without a top for the royal grandson.' We wept bitterly and embraced one another. I was assisted through the Ch'ŏnghwi Gate to the Chŏsŭng-jŏn Mansion, where the palanquin was waiting at the guard gate. Governess Yun accompanied me in the palanquin, which was carried by court guards and followed by a crowd of court maids — an unheard of sight. I had fainted when I got into the palanquin, but was revived by Governess Yun massaging me. When I reached home, I was laid down to rest in a room opposite the main room, while the royal grandson was brought in escorted by my uncle and brother, and the royal grandson's wife and Ch'ŏngyŏn were brought in a palanquin sent from the home of the former. It was such a distressing sight that I felt I could not go on living! However, on reconsideration, I concluded that I had not been successful in killing myself before and that I could not leave the royal grandson to endure such agony alone, for then there would be no one to help him to fulfil his promise. So I continued to suffer the pain of living out my cruel life, and calling on heaven for help. I do not think that anyone since ancient times can have led such a bitter existence.

When I met the royal grandson at my old home I found him most distressed at undergoing such a dreadful experience while still so young. Since I was very worried that he might fall sick from shock, I tried to hide my own true feelings and said, 'Though what has happened is really terrible, it is the will of heaven. Take great care of yourself and be good, and then the state will be peaceful and you will be able to repay royal favours. I know you must be very upset, but take care of yourself so that you come to no harm.'

Since father could not leave the court, and my brother too held a government post which meant staying at court, there was no one at home but my uncle and two of my mother's brothers to attend the royal grandson. They looked after him, attending him day and night, while my youngest brother, who used to play with the royal grandson whenever he came to court as a child, slept in the male guest room together with him. After about a week the board minister, Kim Si-mok, and his son, Kim Ki-dae, came to visit us at home. Since our house was quite cramped, and all the court maids belonging to the royal grandson and his wife were there, we rented the house of Yi Kyŏng-ok (an official of the *Hongmun'gwan*[7]) which was situated outside the south wall of our house, and Madame Kim, the wife of the board minister, came there with her daughter-in-law to attend upon the royal grandson's wife. A hole was made in the fence, and they came in and went out through that.

Then father, who had been removed from office and had been staying for some time in the eastern suburbs while the king disposed of the prince's body, was reinstated as senior vice president of the council when the situation was completely hopeless.[8] On hearing the news about the prince, father rushed in a frenzy into the court and fainted on his arrival. The royal grandson, who heard of this while in the prince's attendance room, sent tranquillizing drugs for my father to take. On regaining consciousness, he too had no further desire to live but, like me, he was concerned to look after the royal grandson so that he might not follow in the prince's footsteps. The gods of heaven and earth can bear witness to his utter devotion to the good of the kingdom. Though it was his cruel fate to continue to live, he could hardly do so with equanimity in view of what had happened.

O Yu-sŏn and Pak Sŏng-wŏn came to our gate to request the royal grandson to prostrate himself on a mat and ask for punishment. Of course, it was proper for him to do so, but as he was too young he remained in the small back room. I had been unable to see father since I came home, which made me feel even worse, but the next day father returned with the royal instructions. My son and I shed bitter tears and embraced father as he delivered the king's instructions that I should protect and look after the royal grandson. Even in my overwrought condition I was much moved at hearing this royal edict. I congratulated the royal grandson on obtaining the king's favour, covering his head and saying, 'As your father's wife and son, both of us have borne up against this disaster. So we should never reproach or blame anyone, but only lament our own misfortunes. It is the royal favour alone that has saved our lives on this occasion, and the king is the only one on whom we can rely in the future. Therefore, I wish you to do your best to obey the king, repay his favour, and fulfil your filial duty to your father, by steadying your mind and, most importantly, by leading a good life.' I expressed my gratitude for the royal favour and told father, 'Please tell the king that I owe the rest of my life to him and that I am at his command.' I did not speak deceitfully, since while it was unfortunate that the prince had ever begun to demonstrate such peculiar behaviour patterns, no one was to blame that they developed to the stage they did. For I had no grudge against the king and never dared to blame him.

When father came home from the court he clasped the royal grandson to him, weeping, and comforted him, saying, 'The king is right — be sage and wise so that you can repay his royal favour, and fulfil your filial duty to your father.' Then he returned to court again.

As the days went by I lay in bed in a vague and confused state of mind, unable to imagine the prince's horrible situation. I heard that on 6 July the king had returned to the upper palace, leaving the grain box very tightly shut and buried deep beneath the grass, and that was the end of it. As there was no way of obtaining the material from the court, father himself prepared the burial clothing, and did this with such feeling that he evidently bore no lingering grudges. For many years during the prince's illness, father had supplied him with innumerable sets of clothes, and now he prepared all the burial clothes as a final act of affection for the prince.

On 11 July, at about four o'clock in the afternoon, it rained heavily and thunder rolled across the sky. I recalled that the prince was scared of thunder claps, and wondered what had happened to him, but my imagination was inadequate. I often felt like starving myself or drowning in deep water, or considered strangling myself with a towel. I often clasped a knife in my hand, but could never make the final decision, being weak-willed. So I survived, even though I ate nothing nor drank even water or thin rice gruel. On the night of 11 July I was told that it was all over with the prince. When I thought that he must have been at the point of death as it rained, I could not imagine how he endured such a death, and my whole body was racked with resentment. How cruel and hard it was to survive him!

Though it was the duty of Lady Sŏnhŭi to advise the king to take such measures, and for the king to dispose of the prince, I had expected that they would have felt sorry for him, and bestowed on him the favour of keeping to the traditional mourning attire. But even after that final step, the king was still very angry, and put the *kisaeng*, with whom the prince had been intimate, to death, as well as the eunuch, Pak P'il-su, and court guards, workmen and shamans. This of course was proper and something that I would not dare to criticize. The one thing that I really resent is the matter of the mourning clothes. Because of the prince's clothing phobia, he had been in a habit of trying on many outfits until he felt satisfied with one, and on the day that he was summoned before the king he was in fact wearing a robe of raw cotton cloth. The king, who had been used to seeing the prince in ceremonial or royal robes, now saw the prince in a raw cotton robe for the first time, and not knowing anything of his illness, exclaimed, 'How dare you wear a raw cotton mourning robe. Are you intending to kill me?' He felt there could be no further excuses, and asked that all the prince's belongings be brought in. There was nothing you could not find among them, right down to a military flag. To my amazement, the prince had had several mourner's staffs[9] made, although people are supposed to have only one, even at a state funeral. The prince happened by chance to have made something which looked like a mourner's staff, which he used to carry about with him. He once showed it to me and I was quite shocked to see that grim thing. It was there amongst the things which he had hoarded, which were brought out. The king was so horrified by this, that it was impossible for anyone to discuss the traditional system of mourning with him in connection with the prince. Knowing nothing about the prince's illness, the king attributed everything to the lack of filial piety which had always rankled with him.

At first, the court ministers and officials were going to follow the traditional mourning, but they were not permitted to do so either. However, the king had been benevolent enough to save the royal grandson. Nevertheless, as he had been predisposed to do this because of his illness, in view of the fact that the prince had been deputizing for the king for fourteen years, it would have redounded to the virtue of the king if he and all his subjects had followed the traditional system of mourning. It was very sad that this was not done.

It had been announced on 11 July that the prince was dead, but no one could prepare the various articles required for the period between death and burial, since the king had not restored him posthumously to his former rank. The king felt hesitant to follow the usual custom and reinstate the prince, but on the night of 12 July he posthumously reinstated him as crown prince, and the court ministers held a special meeting and arranged the whole funeral procedure. At first the king suggested that the body should be kept at the Yongdong-gung Palace. Father, who had witnessed the whole horrible disaster, was too terrified to oppose the king in any way, for the royal anger was then like a flame, and my whole family could easily have been consumed. More importantly, it would have been difficult to guarantee the safety of the royal grandson. Therefore father, acting in all loyalty and sincerity, did his best not to upset the king or turn against the prince or arouse the resentment of the royal grandson, and so arranged everything. Afterwards, when the king granted the prince a posthumous title, he set aside the royal institute of the crown prince as the last resting place for the body, and was persuaded to establish three temporary offices of government.[10] Father himself became a minister of these offices, and took personal charge of everything concerning the funeral: even the etiquette at the tomb was taken care of by him. If it had not been for father's intervention, no one would have dared to say a word to the king or have tried to persuade him to change his mind.

That day, father moved the body to the royal institute of the crown prince. He came home early in the morning, and before escorting us back to court, held my hands as we stood in the middle of the courtyard and weeping bitterly, said, 'May you live long with the royal grandson and enjoy immense happiness in your old age!' I felt that since ancient times no one could have experienced such sorrow. After we returned to court, I announced the death at Simin-dang Hall, as did the royal grandson at Kŏndŏk-hap Pavilion. The wife of the royal grandson and Princess Ch'ŏngyŏn, who was standing beside me, followed suit — such a sight had never been seen before! All the robes required for the funeral and the whole period of mourning were prepared, and the body dressed. I was told that, although it was then extremely hot, the prince's body was not in the least offensive.

I am unable to recall how distressed I was at that time. After the prince was washed and clothed, and before they bound him with hempcloth, I presented myself and experienced a sorrow unequalled in all the past. I recalled the words spoken by the prince, and full of regret at being still alive, called out to heaven. Since this world is separated from the other world, I could not feel that robust strength of his, and so cannot explain my feeling of resentment at being alive. I was very depressed throughout the funeral, especially since the junior officials were not allowed to follow the traditional mourning, and all the officials of the main palace and eunuchs were clothed in pale blue sacrificial robes. The sacrificial rites were performed at the outer palace where the body was lying, but there had been no notice from the king about performing the ritual in the inner courtyard, and so this ritual was not conducted. However, the morning and evening sacrificial meals were offered every day and the sacrificial rituals on the first and fifteenth day of the month were performed as usual.

Since the royal grandson and his wife and the princesses could not for all the world be allowed to see the body before it was placed in the coffin, we permitted them to come in and mourn on the first day of wearing mourning robes.[11] Everybody was moved by the intensity of the royal grandson's grief. The burial took place on 10 September 1762. Prior to that Lady Sŏnhǔi had come to see me. She faced the room where the body lay and wept bitterly, beating her head and breast with her hands. She was very distressed.

At the burial the king came to the tomb and wrote the letters (counter for the souls of the dead) on the ancestral tablet in person. I could not imagine what their relationship would be, now that the prince and his father lived in two different worlds. That same month, the royal institute of the crown prince was established and the royal grandson became the crown prince. Though this honour was due to royal favour, it indicated my father's loyal efforts to protect the royal grandson.

In the eighth month, the king came to the Sŏnwŏn-jŏn Shrine for the simple sacrificial rites, and I decided to go to the Supch'wi-hŏn Audience Chamber near the Sŏnwŏn-jŏn Shrine and meet him, even though I was still uncertain about my feelings. I said to the king, without revealing the full depth of my sorrow, 'It was thanks to Your Highness' royal favour that both mother and children have been preserved.'

King Yŏngjo grasped my hands in his and said, weeping, 'It was a hard decision for me to see you, for I did not think you would behave like this. It is very good of you to put me at my ease like this.' The cruel fact that it was I who was alive to hear these royal words made me feel as if I were suffocating.

'I wish Your Highness would take the royal grandson with you to the Kyŏnghŭi Palace and instruct him yourself,' I continued.

'Do you think he can bear to live apart from you?' the king asked.

'It is a small thing for him to feel sad because he is living away from me, whereas it is very important for him to study in the company of Your Highness,' I answered. For I had just reached the sudden decision to send the royal grandson away, although it would be difficult for myself as his mother to part with my child.

It was hard for the royal grandson to leave me and he eventually left in tears. I had to go on living, while feeling as if my heart was torn in two. In the meantime, the royal grandson was showered with the royal favour and love, and Lady Sŏnhŭi also transferred her love for her son to her grandson. As was only natural, she fussed over him protectively, never feeling quite satisfied about his daily behaviour and meals. Since the royal grandson had been devoted to studying the classics since the age of four or five, I did not worry that he might not concentrate on his studies, though we lived in separate palaces. But he missed me more and more as time went by. His longing for me was so strong that he used to wake up early in the morning, and set his mind at rest by writing to me in order to get my answer back before he started his studies. He was like that for the whole three years of our separation, which was remarkably precocious of him. And moreover, as I was very often sick during those three years, he would discuss my health with the royal physician and prepare the medicine for me like an adult. This was, of course, all due to his innate filial piety, but even so I was really moved to see him managing all this when barely more than ten years of age.[12]

I did not feel like going out on the prince's birthday that year, but could not avoid going to the upper palace in obedience to the royal command. I was received by the king, who was even more sympathetic to me than before, and gave the name of *Kahyodang*[13] to the low hut on the south side of the Kyŏngch'un-jŏn Mansion, where I was living while in mourning. He wrote the name on the board in person, and asked that it be put above the door, saying, 'I am writing this to repay you for your filial piety.' I choked back my tears and felt that I ought not to receive it.

Father was very pleased to hear about this and said, 'This board on which the king today wrote the letters *Kahyodang* will be a treasure for our descendants. I admire both the benevolence of the king, and your filial piety in holding the royal favours in such great esteem.' Father had our family use that title on all the family letters, in order to show due respect for this royal favour. My own gratitude went so deep that it was engraved on my bones.

The king had the Chagyŏng-jŏn Mansion built for me, but I felt my situation then was not such as to allow me to live in a high and grandiose residence. However, I was moved by the royal favour, and so complied with the king's wishes. Feeling that this was where I would spend the rest of my life, I moved the *Kahyodang* board to the south gate of the upper room in the Chagyŏng-jŏn Mansion, so that I might always remember the king's great benevolence and compassion.

In the twelfth month, 1762, an envoy came from China, and the king and the royal grandson accompanied him to the crown prince's shrine to receive the imperial edict. On their return, the king was intending to take the royal grandson back with him. But when he saw the boy crying because he was unhappy about leaving his mother, he said to me, 'I will leave the royal grandson with you, since he cannot bear to leave you.'

Thinking that the king might feel offended when, despite all his love for his grandson, the boy rejected the royal favour out of longing for his mother, I said, 'If he should come to me, he will miss Your Highness; if he goes to Your Highness, he will miss me. So please take him with you, since he will feel just like this about being away from Your Highness.'

The king appeared very gratified, and with a pleased look took the royal grandson with him, saying, 'Very well, I shall do so then.'

The royal grandson went back with the king, crying bitterly at his mother's apparent lack of feeling in forcing him to leave. I felt very dejected, but it would have been giving in to personal emotions for him to get off the palanquin then, whereas it was right for him to escort the king back to the palace, succeeding to those offices and duties of a son which his father had been unable to fulfil, and being trained in affairs of state. This is why I cut the bond of feeling between us and sent him away. I deeply regretted all that had happened in the past, and wanted to let the royal grandson fulfil his filial duties toward the king, as his father had failed to do. Also, I was most concerned that the royal grandson might contravene, even in the slightest, the royal favour. Such considerations were based not only on my own personal feelings for him, but because the future security of the kingdom depended entirely on the royal grandson. Heaven, therefore, would have seen my concern as right. Of course, the idea did not originate from me alone, for father guided me in everything and urged me not to allow my trivial personal feelings as a mother to influence me, but rather to face up to the demands of duty. No one could possibly imagine the extent to which father devoted himself to the interest of the royal grandson and the kingdom.

Everyone was moved by the sound of the royal grandson's lamentations, whenever he visited his father's shrine. The ancestral tablet which stood there on its own stand seemed to be very glad to see the prince's son come and lament over his death, and the lonely shrine seemed to be infused with an atmosphere which comforted the mourner. What would have happened to the kingdom if I had not given birth to the royal grandson? But of course there was the happy event of 1752, when the royal grandson was born, a year after I had given birth to a child in 1750, to preserve the declining kingdom.

The Imo Incident was something the like of which had never been seen since ancient times, and the crown prince was indeed extremely unfortunate to finish his life in such a way. Yet he left a son behind to succeed him. The king's favour towards the royal grandson and the latter's filial piety toward his grandfather were intimately linked, so that I never imagined there would be any further problems. Consequently, the king's action of March 1764 was so utterly unexpected that my feelings of the time were without comparison, though as a subject I should not complain of what the king did.[14] I really resented having to survive this incident, and being unable to kill myself. Though I wanted to kill myself immediately, I could not do so and had to endure what took place as if it had happened through my own will. My feelings of resentment were not less than those I experienced in a certain year (year Imo), and the Lady Sŏnhŭi's mortification was beyond description.

The royal grandson, who had suffered so much agony as a very young child and who had experienced calamities such as a member of a royal family should never have suffered, was extremely sad and cried bitterly when he took off his mourner's robe. His lamentations must have penetrated heaven and earth. His sorrow then was not less intense than that which he first displayed at his father's death. He was then two years older, and feeling more resentful as time passed. This distressed me so much, that I wanted to kill myself straight away, but I could not do so for fear of the royal grandson's reaction. Without me, he would be left all alone and very insecure and so my most important task at this stage was to protect him. I took a firm stance and attempted to comfort him, saying, 'The more you feel sad, the better you should protect your precious self. Even though you feel very resentful, be good and make amends for your father.' So I calmed the royal grandson, helping him as best I could. He wept all day and would not eat, endangering his health. I felt so sorry for him that I let him lie beside me, hoping to soothe him to sleep. However, he was too upset to sleep and it was indescribable.

The day was 23 March 1764, and I still wonder why the king could have done such a thing. On that day, King Yŏngjo suddenly proceeded to Sŏnwŏn-jŏn Shrine, where he stayed for some time before coming to see me. I, of course, dared to say nothing except, 'Though you have acted in this way, it is not for me to complain, since it is on account of the royal favour that we, the mother and child, are still alive.'

The king said, 'It is right of you to think that way.' It would have been easier for me if I had not had to experience this further resentment on top of my grief. The passing of time revealed my life to be more and more ill-fated, so that I felt like hitting myself — but what is the use of it!

During the seventh month, Lady Sŏnhŭi came to perform the ritual marking the second anniversary of the death of the crown prince, and promised me that she would certainly come to stay with us after the autumn and discuss the king's action. However, to my great distress, she developed a malignant tumour on her back and passed away on 23 August. The sorrow I felt was not such as might have stemmed from a normal relationship between mother-in-law and daughter-in-law. For the sake of the kingdom, Lady Sŏnhŭi had taken the most awful step that a mother could take. Although she did it for King Yŏngjo, her utmost agony was beyond description. She used to say, 'Since I have done such a thing — something I should have never dared to do — even the grass will not grow on my grave.' Or 'although I did it for the kingdom and the king himself, it was cruel and terrible of me. You may perhaps understand me, but what will the royal grandson and his sisters think of me?' She could hardly sleep at night, and would sit on the east side of the verandah, gazing towards the east and grieving, reflecting that the kingdom might have been saved even if she had not taken such a step and perhaps she could have been mistaken. And then she would tell herself, no, thinking in such a way was to display the mind of a weak woman, and she must have done the right thing. Whenever she came to the shrine, she would weep bitterly. This eventually caused an illness in her heart which led to her death. Alas! it was really sad to think of.

Is there anyone today who knows better than I what happened in that terrible year; who had devoted himself or herself so sincerely and utterly to the prince; or whose sadness can be compared to that of myself and King Chŏngjo? There is no one. So it was that I always told King Chŏngjo, 'Though you are the prince's son, you were quite young when the Incident occurred; you can hardly know as much as I. So please ask me about it if there is anything you want to know; do not put your faith in various rumours. People collect such stories and report them to you as if they are great discoveries, in order to insinuate themselves into your favour. Please do not trust them, for they are groundless.'

Then my son would answer, 'Mother, of course I know that, but when they continually say that I am just the victim's son, or accuse me of not being really devoted to my father, I ought to avoid blame. Though I was sure they were wrong, I have followed their suggestion and have never been able to assert that they were wrong, honouring those whom they recommended or giving them posthumous titles. This way I could show them that I was not such a waverer as they claimed, though I knew clearly that they were in the wrong.' It is difficult to imagine his agony of mind.

There are two different stories abroad, generally speaking, about the Incident, and both of them are false and dishonest. One is that it was fair and just for King Yŏngjo to do what he did, and that his actions were justified before heaven and earth. Those who take this view have no pity at all for the prince; rather they admired King Yŏngjo's action as an example of flourishing virtue. This view assumes that the prince was guilty of unfilial conduct towards his father, so that King Yŏngjo's action is considered in the same light as devastating an enemy country or suppressing a rebellion. Thus, both the prince and King Yŏngjo are put in an unreal situation, an equally unfortunate result for both.

The other view is that the prince in fact was not sick at all, and that King Yŏngjo took these extreme measures against him, through placing reliance upon a false charge. These people tried to persuade King Chŏngjo to take revenge in order to clear his father's name. While their intention may have been to clear the prince's name, this argument meant that King Yŏngjo had simply accepted false charges and proceeded against the prince when he was not guilty. In such a case, King Yŏngjo would appear to have lost his virtue. Therefore, I say that both of the views are false, and would make all three, King Yŏngjo, the prince and King Chŏngjo, extremely sad.

This was why my father insisted over and over again that because the prince's illness had become so very serious, the king and the kingdom were in immense danger, and their fortunes hung on a breath. King Yŏngjo had to take such a step, and the prince, when he was sane, would have felt disgusted with his immorality, but he lost his true self and did not feel that way. In the first place, the fact that he became sick was totally disastrous. It is said that even a saint cannot avoid being sick, so how could anyone accuse the prince of being even in the slightest immoral? This being so, it should be fairly recognized that King Yŏngjo's action was justified and inevitable, though it was very unfortunate. As the prince had become so sick, there was no other way than for him to be eliminated in this manner. So King Chŏngjo ought to have distinguished between his emotions and his sense of duty and viewed the Incident for what it was, as a reasonable display of his sense of duty. However, the previous two views make King Yŏngjo lose his virtue and the prince immoral, thus putting King Chŏngjo in a dreadful situation.

Some of those who have discussed the matter say that King Yŏngjo's action was glorious. They claim that my father gave the grain box to the king and therefore he was guilty of the prince's death. I will not explain the details again, for I have already put them on record. Those who speak in this way can be neither sincere to King Yŏngjo nor loyal to the prince. They know that as far as the Incident was concerned, King Chŏngjo would listen to anybody without criticism, not being able to refute them. Accordingly, they misused the Incident by forging a false story and affair, wilfully harming those people with pretensions of loyalty. There was never such a thing from ancient times. For forty years that Incident has been used to confuse loyalty and treachery, right and wrong, and even yet the matter has not been sorted out. Nothing could have helped the prince's illness. King Yŏngjo's action was inevitable. The final scene was devised by King Yŏngjo himself. The agony of loss and the sense of duty should be confined to King Chŏngjo and myself alone, for it is we who should be grateful for the royal favour which preserved us and eventually maintained the kingdom so long free from disaster.

I feel unhappy when I think that later generations have misunderstood the Incident, through trying to imagine the words and actions of the people involved, who were placed in an unavoidable situation. As far as the Incident is concerned, no one, be he king or subject, should be allowed to make any comment. Although I have no wish to record the details of the Incident, I am doing so because I am concerned lest King Sunjo should not know the true facts, and that he might not be able to tell right from wrong. However, there are many many things I have not written here, for they are too awful to be recorded. It is quite amazing how cruel, tough and evil human beings can be. When I reflect that I have been able to record all this during my old age, with white hair and little of my life left before me, I simply feel resentful of my fate, weep bitter tears and call upon heaven.

Appendix I: Biographical Index

This is an index of the principal characters mentioned in the text. For the reader's convenience, names of particular persons are entered under one name following the entries in the *Encyclopedia of Korean History* and standard Korean histories. In the original text, several alternative names are often given for the same person, but in such cases only the standard name has been given in this text, as above. Women in Korea officially had only one name (surname) which was their maiden name, and which they kept after their marriage. But they are sometimes referred to in the text by surname and name of origin.

LADY CHANG ?–1701
> The mother of King Kyongjong, 20th King of the Yi dynasty, and royal concubine of King Sukjong, 19th King.

CROWN PRINCE CHANGHŎN: See Crown Prince Sado.

MADAME CHŎNG 1738–?
> The ninth daughter of King Yŏngjo by Lady Sŏnhŭi. She was widowed without a son when very young and adopted Chŏng Hu-gyŏm as her son. She spent most of her time in the palace after her husband's death and enjoyed the king's special favour. She was later dismissed from the

111

royal family, sent into exile to a remote place and then poisoned on the orders of King Chŏngjo, her nephew. This was why the authoress described her as Madame Chŏng instead of Princess Hwawan. The authoress hinted at incest between her husband, the crown prince and her sister-in-law Madame Chŏng, which I believe was the main cause of King Yŏngjo's decision to kill his son, the crown prince, and later King Chŏngjo's decision to poison his aunt.

CHŎNG HU-GYŎM

Adopted son of Madame Chŏng.

KING CHŎNGJO Reigned 1776–1800

The 22nd King of the Yi dynasty. He was the grandson of King Yŏngjo and the second son of Crown Prince Sado and the authoress. Following his father's tragic death, he became crown prince and eventually succeeded King Yŏngjo to the throne. King Chŏngjo was an able man and as fine a scholar as any of his officials. However, he was engrossed with learning and devoid of interest in politics, entrusting the care of the government to the chief royal secretary. He established the royal research institute, where the scholars of the state gathered to discuss the classics and histories of ancient China. With his encouragement they published numerous valuable books. He was very resentful of his father's tragic death, and in his memory built a new city wall around Suwon, promoted it to a minor capital, and made regular visits there.

QUEEN CHŎNGSŎNG 1692–1757

The first wife of King Yŏngjo. She was childless.

QUEEN CHŎNGSUN 1745–1805

The second wife of King Yŏngjo. She was childless, did not get along well with Prince Sado, and maligned him a great deal. When young King Sunjo succeeded to the throne after the death of King Chŏngjo she manipulated the government from behind the scenes.

PRINCESS CH'ŎNGYŎN 1754–?
The first daughter of the authoress and the crown prince.

LADY HONG OF HYEGYŎNG PALACE 1735-1815
The authoress of this book and the wife of Crown Prince Sado. She was the daughter of the president of the council, Hong Pong-han, and mother of King Chŏngjo. In King Kojong's (r. 1863–1907) day, her husband Crown Prince Sado was posthumously conferred King Changjo and accordingly she was also elevated as Queen Kyŏngŭi. When King Chŏngjo succeeded to the throne, he honoured his mother with the title Hyegyŏng-gung. She had a son and two daughters.

HONG PONG-HAN 1713–1778
The father of the authoress. He passed the higher civil service examination in 1744 and was appointed councillor of the frontier defence command in 1754; president of the council in 1761. However, he was removed from office for a while because of the king's suspicions of Crown Prince Sado and reappointed senior vice president of the council in 1763.

PRINCESS HWAHYŎP
The seventh daughter of King Yŏngjo by Lady Sŏnhŭi. Though she was exceptionally beautiful, she, like her brother, Crown Prince Sado, was never favoured by her father.

PRINCESS HWAP'YŎNG ?–1748
The third daughter of King Yŏngjo by Lady Sŏnhŭi. She was one of the daughters King Yŏngjo loved most. She died in childbirth in 1748.

PRINCESS HWASUN
The second daughter of King Yŏngjo by Lady Yŏnu.

PRINCESS HWAWAN: See Madame Chŏng.

CROWN PRINCE HYOJANG: See Prince Kyongui.

QUEEN HYOSUN 1715–1751
The wife of Crown Prince Hyojang. She was childless.

QUEEN HYOŬI 1753–1821
The wife of King Chŏngjo. She was childless.

QUEEN INWŎN 1687–1757
The third wife of King Sukjong and stepmother of King Yŏngjo. She was childless.

PRINCE ILSONG
The husband of Princess Hwawan, Madame Chŏng.

LADY KASUN: See Lady Pak of Kasun Palace.

KIM SANG-NO 1702–?
He passed the higher civil service examination in 1734. He was the minister of the board of revenue, the junior vice president of the council and president of the council. After his death, King Chŏngjo withdrew his posthumous title, sent his two sons into exile and made his grandson a slave because King Chŏngjo believed that Kim Sang-no had alienated Crown Prince Sado from his father, King Yŏngjo.

PRINCE KŬMSŎNG
The husband of Princess Hwap'yŏng, the third daughter of King Yŏngjo.

KYŎNGMO-GUNG: See Crown Prince Sado.

PRINCE KYŎNGŬI 1719–1728
The first son of King Yŏngjo. He died at the age of ten.

LADY PAK OF KASUN PALACE 1770–1822
The mother of King Sunjo and concubine of King Chŏngjo.

THE ROYAL GRANDSON: See King Chŏngjo.

CROWN PRINCE SADO 1735–1762
The second son of King Yŏngjo by Lady Sŏnhŭi. He was

114

appointed crown prince in 1735 and deputized for the king from 1749, but fell sick and behaved eccentrically. He was killed by his father, who locked him in a grain box in 1762.

SIN MAN 1703–?

Passed the higher civil service examination in 1726. He was the minister of the board of war, minister of the board of civil office and the junior vice president of the council. He became president of the council in 1762.

KING SUNJO, reigned 1801–1834

The 23rd King of Yi dynasty. He was the second son of King Chŏngjo by Lady Pak of Kasun Palace. During his reign the powerful *Yangban* officials, by entering into marriage alliances with the sovereign, were able to ensure for themselves a firm grasp on political power, so that every important national policy formulated in this period took their interest, and the maintenance of their power into account. However King Sunjo made a major contribution to social reform, and to the development of Korean culture and institutions in the latter Yi period. In 1801, for the first time, the Korean monarchy took oppressive measures against the Catholics.

PRINCE WŎLSŎNG

The husband of Princess Hwasun.

LADY YI OF HANSAN

The authoress' mother.

KING YŎNGJO, reigned 1725–1776

The 21st King of Yi dynasty. He was the fourth son of King Sukjong. As soon as he ascended the throne, he attempted to end factional strife because he was aware of its detrimental effects on state administration. His principal policy to end factional splits was expressed in the slogan 'peace prevails while a monarch administers with objective non-partisanship'. He amended the recruitment of officials of the office of study promotion from the system of recommendation to one of voting. Before re-applying the shortlived universal military service tax, he went out of the palace gate and asked the opinion of officials, literati, soldiers and peasants. He then reduced the military service tax of two *p'il* of cloth by half, and ordered this deficiency supplemented by taxes on fishing, salt and increased land tax. He also reorganized the state's revenue and expenditure by adopting an accounting system. He minted coins to encourage the circulation of currency.

His concern for the improvement of peasant life was manifested in his eagerness to educate the people by distributing important books in Korean script. He also reinstated the drumbeat appeal for spontaneous petitioning. Further, he eliminated medieval types of punishment and torture. He warned the *Yangban* against luxurious living and stopped the accumulation of wealth by excessive exploitation. He also established a special state examination for old people (*Kirokkwa*). Literati and soldiers of 60 years and above sat for this examination and those who passed were appointed government officials.

Under him the pluviometer was again manufactured in quantity and distributed to local officials to encourage agricultural efficiency. He also undertook public works, mobilizing 200,000 persons for a two-month period to dredge river beds. This work was made into a regular public service by the establishment of the office of dredge works. All his efforts and policies were intended to reassert the Confucian monarchy and humanitarian rule. His reign, together with that of his grandson Chŏngjo, was the golden age of the latter Yi dynasty. However, his reforms aimed at preserving dynastic rule could not succeed against the tide of rapidly changing society. Nevertheless, his reign was the longest of all the Yi dynasty kings.

PRINCE YŎNGSŎNG

Princess Hwahyŏp's husband. He was the son of the president of the council, Sin Man.

Appendix II: Maps

Seoul, the capital of the country during the Yi dynasty, had five royal palaces: the Ch'an'gyŏng, Ch'angdŏk, Kyŏngbok, Tŏksu and Kyŏnghŭi palaces. Four of them still exist, although so much changed that it is very difficult to visualize their original structure.

Out of these five palaces, only three are mentioned in the text, the Kyŏnghŭi, Ch'an'gyŏng and Ch'angdŏk. The Kyŏnghŭi Palace was built in 1616, but completely disappeared. It was a great palace of more than a hundred separate buildings. After 1910, it was dismantled by the Japanese, and most of the buildings either became Japanese shrines, private property, or were destroyed. The Japanese High School, now the Seoul High School, was built on the site of a demolished section of this palace.

The Ch'an'gyŏng was originally built in 1419 and called the Sugang Palace. It was given its new name when rebuilt in 1483 and became used as a zoo and a botanical garden from the end of the Yi dynasty.

The Ch'angdŏk was built in 1404. It was completely burnt down by the Japanese invaders in 1592 except for the Tonhwa Gate. It was rebuilt in 1611.

The two last-named palaces still exist today and can easily be seen by visitors to Seoul.

In addition to these royal palaces, there were two important temple compounds often mentioned in the text: the Royal Ancestral Temple of the Yi dynasty royal family; and the Seven Temples, where the ancestral tablets of royal mothers without the title of queen were kept.

117

Map I shows the location of these two palaces and two shrines.
Map II shows the location of separate buildings of the Ch'an'gyŏng Palace.
Map III shows the same details of the Ch'angdŏk Palace. As a result of its destruction, no map can be provided of the Kyŏnghŭi Palace.

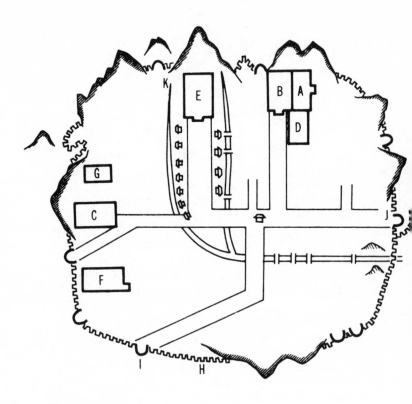

MAP I: OLD SEOUL

MAP I: OLD SEOUL

Five royal palaces, Royal Ancestral Temple, National Shrine and Capital Fortress

A. Ch'ang'gyŏng Palace
B. Ch'angdŏk Palace
C. Kyŏnghŭi Palace
D. Royal Ancestral Temple
E. Kyŏngbok Palace
F. Tŏksu Palace

G. National Shrine
H. Capital Fortress
I. Sŭngnye Gate (present South
J. Gate)
K. Hŭngin Gate (present East Gate)
   Seven Temples

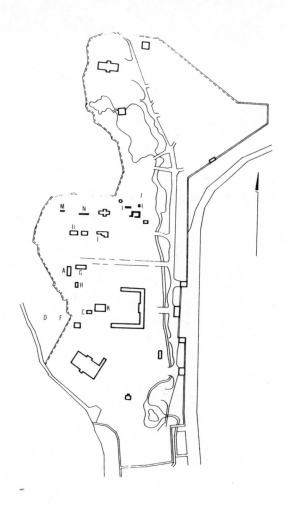

MAP II: CH'AN'GYŎNG PALACE

A. Kyŏngch'un-jŏn Mansion
B. T'onmyŏng-jŏn Mansion
C. Sŭngmun-dang Hall
D. Old Chŏsŭng-jŏn Mansion site
E. Chippok-hŏn Side Apartment
F. Naksŏnjae Library
G. Hwan'gyŏng-jŏn Mansion

H. Hamin-jŏng Pavilion
I. Kosŏ-hon Side Apartment
J. Kŏn'guk-dang Hall
K. Myŏngjŏn-jŏn Mansion
L. Nanhyang-gak Audience Chamber
M. Old Hwanch'wi-jŏn Mansion site
N. Old Chagyŏng-jŏn Mansion site

MAP III: CH'ANGDŎK PALACE

A. Injŏng-jŏn Mansion
B. Taejo-jŏn Mansion
C. Yun'gyŏng-jŏn Mansion
D. Hŭijŏng-jŏn Mansion
E. Old Kŏnyang Gate

F. Kyŏnghŭng-gak Audience
   Chamber
G. Old Yŏngmo-dang Hall site
H. Old Kyŏngbok-jŏn Mansion site
I. Manan Gate
J. Sŏnwŏn Hall

120

The Relations of Crown Prince Sado

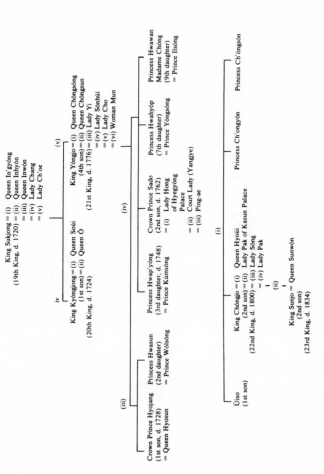

Notes

Chapter I

1. The noted president of the council in King Yŏngjo's day, Yun Tu-su (1533–1601). Pen-name, O-ŭm.
2. A title given to a person who has passed only the first test of the minor state examination.
3. A title given to a person who has passed the Confucian classics at the final test of the minor state examination (Esquire, Esq.). The Confucian classics and poetry and composition were the subjects for the final test.
4. *The Book of Moral Training* compiled by Liu Tzu-ch'eng following the instructions of Chu Tzu in 1187. It was soon introduced to Korea and used as a text-book for moral training and as an elementary book of Confucian studies for children of about eight years.
5. The wife of the Crown Prince Hyojang, the first son of King Yŏngjo.
6. One of the four political factions of the middle period of the Yi dynasty.
7. Seaweed soup and rice. It was, and still is, Korean custom for mothers to eat seaweed soup and rice at every meal after the delivery of a baby.
8. The author's father was the president of the council at that time.
9. The Confucian Academy.
10. Famous letter of loyalty written by Chu Ko-liang (181–234) to his young Emperor Liu Shan (Hu-chu, 207–271) of the Shu Han kingdom during his military expedition to Wei. (See Lu Pi, San kuo chihchi-chieh: Shu Chih, ch.5, pp. 15–18.)

123

Chu Ko-liang was principal advisor of Liu Pei (221–223), founder of the Shu-Han (the Three Kingdoms) and regent for his son. He is one of the main characters of the Chinese novel *San-kuo-chih yen i* by Lo Kuan-chung (ca 1330–ca 1400).

[11] Cho Kwan-bin disobeyed the royal command to compose and present the official document of record affirming the investiture of the consort of the crown prince.

[12] *Classic of Filial Piety* a compilation of filial piety doctrines by Confucius and Tseng Tzu.

[13] When the author lost her eldest son.

[14] The birth of the author's second son, the future King Chŏngjo.

[15] See pp. 58–63.

[16] Princess Hwawan.

[17] These events and their background form the principal subject of Chapters II and III.

Chapter II

[1] The first son and heir of King Yŏngjo.

[2] A legendary Chinese ruler of remote antiquity credited with the invention of the figures known as the eight trigrams, on which the Confucian classic and manual of divination of the Yi dynasty is based.

[3] A title given to the officials of the royal institute.

[4] The royal institute of the crown prince and the office of the royal bodyguard for the crown prince.

[5] The second wife of King Sukjong. She married King Sukjong and became queen in 1689. For a long time King Sukjong had no son, so when Lady Chang gave birth to his child Kyun in 1688, the king tried to appoint him crown prince. But the Westerners (*Sŏin*) who had a firm grasp on political power at that time did not agree with the king, saying that since the queen was still young, it would be better to wait longer. With the help of the Southerners (*Namin*) however, the king appointed Kyun crown prince and elevated Chang So-ŭi to Lady Chang in 1689. In the same year, the king dismissed Queen Inhyŏn because of the false charges of Lady Chang and appointed the latter queen. But later the king regretted that he had dismissed Queen Inhyŏn, and in 1694 he restored her and demoted Lady Chang from queen to her former position. After the death of Queen Inhyŏn, it was learnt that Lady Chang had built a shrine to the west of Ch'wisŏn-dang Hall where she had prayed for the queen's death. She was condemned to death for this.

[6] King Yŏngjo was the half brother of King Kyŏngjong. Queen Ŏ

objected when her husband appointed his brother, later King Yŏngjo, the crown prince.

7   The mother of the Chinese philosopher Mencius is said to have moved house from the neighbourhood of a cemetery when she noticed her son playing at funerals, and later to have moved again from a house near the market when she noticed him playing at shops. Their third home was near a school!

8   One of the numerous titles applied to Crown Prince Sado.

9   This seems to have been the first sign of mental instability. Cf. p. 51–3.

10   *Sin-Im Sahwa*, 1721–1722: this calamity occurred because of factional strife between the *Noron* and *Soron* groups over the succession to the throne in King Kyŏngjong's reign. King Kyŏngjong was childless and had been sick for a long time. The president of the council at that time, Kim Ch'ang-jip, advised the king to appoint Prince Yŏnin and have him deputize for the king. Prince Yŏnin was later King Yŏngjo, and the half-brother of King Kyŏngjong. Prince Yŏnin was thus appointed the crown prince in 1721 (the first year of King Kyŏngjong's reign) and later deputized for the king on Kim Ch'ang-jip's advice. But the junior vice president of the council, Cho T'ae-gu and his *Soron* group successfully impeached Kim Ch'ang-jip and the rest of the ministers, falsely accusing them of various crimes, then sending them into exile and eventually killing them. This upset occurred during the year of *Sinch'uk* and *Imsin*. But as soon as King Yŏngjo succeeded to the throne, the *Soron* group itself was attacked and Kim Il-kyŏng and his fellows were killed. Because of this bitterness, when King Yŏngjo succeeded to the throne, he proclaimed the slogan of 'Non-partisanship' and tried to end this factional feud. Chindan Hakhoe, ed. (Seoul, 1968), *Han'guksa* v. 4, pp. 53–55.

11   *Musin Yŏkpyŏn*: the remnants of the *Soron* group, who felt resentful at what had happened in the *Sin-Im Sahwa*, rose in rebellion in 1728 (*Musin*), the fourth year of King Yŏngjo's reign. Their leaders were Yi In-chwa, Chŏng Hŭi-ryang and others. Chindan Hakchoe, ibid, v. 4, p. 58.

12   Men were recruited through the state examination (*kwagŏ*) system to fill government posts. Examinations were of three kinds, civil, military, and miscellaneous. In addition to these regular examinations, special ones were held on various occasions such as national holidays (*chŏngsi* or *kyŏn'gwa*) or on the occasion of the king visiting the Confucian Academy to participate in the semi-annual rites in honour of Confucius (*alsŏngsi*) etc. Taejŏn hoet'ong. *Kugyŏk taejŏn hoet'ong*, Hanguk-kojŏn kugyok ch'ongso,

vol. 1, Han'guk Kojŏn Kugyŏk Wiwŏnhoe, ed. (Seoul, 1962), p. 248.

13 One for whom objective existences have ceased to be, and in whose mind positive and negative are one; an honourable destination for a Taoist.

14 The *Yu-shu-ching* (*Okch'ugyŏng Scripture of the Jade Pivot*) describes the god of thunder and his role in punishing the evil-doer. It also deals with punishments in the various hells. The work appears to date from the thirteenth century or before.

15 Cf. p. 39–40.

16 *Yangjye*: an official title given to a court lady with the Lower Second Court rank.

17 T'ai-chia was the grandson and successor of King T'ang, founder of the Shiang dynasty in China. He was deposed from the throne for misconduct by the minister I Yin, and restored three years later when he had reformed his behaviour. The incident is discussed in Mencius.

18 The wife of the Crown Prince Hyojang, Queen Hyosun.

Chapter III

1 A vermilion gate was erected in honour of a royal retainer, a filial son, or a virtuous woman.

2 Emperor Shun: a legendary Chinese ruler, a good, wise and extremely filial king, said to have ruled from 2255–2208 B.C.

3 The president of the council, Yi Ch'ŏn-bo, the senior vice president of the council, Yi Hu, and the junior vice president of the council, Min Paek-sang bore the responsibility for the crown prince's misconduct, which had led to wild rumours around the country. They got into such a dilemma over whether to report this to the king that they poisoned themselves. Yi Ch'ŏn-bo killed himself on 9th February 1761, Yi Hu on 8th April 1761 and Min Paek-sang on 21st March 1761. Yijo sillok, *Chosŏn Wangjo sillok*. Kuksa P'yŏnchan Wiwŏnhoe, ed. (Seoul, 1955–58), v. 44, p. 56, 58, 59.

4 Chiang Ch'ung took part in a plot to convince Emperor Wu of Han that his son and heir had been involved in magical practices against him. The unfortunate prince was put to death with his children on 30 September 91 B.C., after he had himself killed Chiang Ch'ung on 1 September. Wang Hsien-ch'ien, *Han shu pu-chu*, v. 45, pp. 39–30 (double leaf).

5 High-class female entertainer.

6 *Na Kyŏng-ŏn ŭi Sangbyŏn*: this Incident occurred on 14 June 1762 when Na Kyŏng-ŏn, a steward of Yun Kŭp, the minister of the board of punishment, sent a memorial to the king informing him

of the misconduct of Crown Prince Sado. The accusations in the memorial were that he had clubbed to death the concubine that gave birth to one of his sons; had violated the court regulations by bringing a nun into the court and cohabiting with her; had visited P'yŏngyang, the chief amusement centre, in disguise; and had frequented the village outside the north gate of Seoul, which was famous as a community of female shamans. When Na Kyŏng-ŏn was questioned about this memorial and tortured to ascertain who had persuaded him to write it, he named Yun Kŭp, Kim Hang-gu and Hong Kye-hŭi. Though King Yŏngjo tried to reprieve Na Kyŏng-ŏn, Nam T'ae-jye and Hong Nak-sun persuaded the king to put him to death for disloyalty to the crown prince. Kuksa P'yonch'an Wiwŏnhoe, ibid. v. 44, pp. 98–99.

7 One of the government offices of the Yi dynasty in which were kept the Confucian classics, historical books and government documents. It housed the royal advisors.

8 On 14 June 1762, the president of the Council, Hong Pong-han, was dismissed from his post in connection with the Na Kyŏng-ŏn Incident. (Kuksa P'yŏnch'an Wiwŏnhoe, ibid., v. 44, p. 99). However, he was reappointed senior vice president of the Council on 28 June, only a fortnight after his dismissal. (Kuksa P'yŏnch'an Wiwŏnhoe, ibid., v. 44, p. 99). He thus held a senior ministerial post at the time the crown prince was put to death, a fact which his daughter here glosses over. The crown prince was dethroned and locked into a grain box on 4 July 1762 and died on 12 July 1762 after seven days of confinement. (Kuksa P'yŏnch'an Wiwŏnhoe, ibid., v. 44, pp. 101–102).

9 The staff is traditionally an essential part of a mourner's attire at a funeral. A bamboo staff is used for a father's funeral and a paulownia one for a mother's.

10 The office in charge of the apartment where corpses were laid in state, the office in charge of state funerals and the office in charge of entombments.

11 Mourning robes are worn from the fourth day following the death.

12 He was actually twelve at this time.

13 'Hall of Admired Filial Piety'.

14 The decision was taken by King Yŏngjo on 22 (23 in the text) March 1764, whereby it was arranged for the royal grandson to be an heir of Crown Prince Hyojang — the king's first son who had died in 1728. Kuksa P'yŏnch'an Wiwŏnhoe, ibid., v. 44, p. 159.